TEN MILES FROM

Front cover photo Taken 1946, shows 'Squibbie' Murkin and 'Waters' Alcock outside the Walnut Tree pub, also known as the Sizzle, at Attleton Green. It is now a private house.

Dedicated to
Wickhambrook Community Association
and the
contributors to the *Wickhambrook Scene*
past and present.

TEN MILES FROM ANYWHERE

A SUFFOLK CHRONICLE

by

John Bean

HEDGEROW PUBLISHING
Newmarket

First published 1995 by
Hedgerow Publishing
East Cottage
Wickhambrook
Newmarket
Suffolk CB8 8YA

ISBN 0-9525440-0-8

British Library Cataloguing in Publication Data
A catalogue record for this book is
available from the British Library

Photoset by Rowland Phototypesetting Limited
Bury St Edmunds, Suffolk
Printed in Great Britain by St Edmundsbury Press Limited
Bury St Edmunds, Suffolk

Foreword

Changing life patterns over the past twenty-five years, not least the development of the motorway system and the increasing stress of city life, have had a profound effect on the English village. In many instances it has been altered completely, with today's descendants of countless rural generations being forced to live in the towns and cities, unable to compete with more affluent towns people in the purchase of the homes where their forbears once lived.

In some cases it has led to the sterile village. Inhabited almost entirely by a mix of daily commuters working in cities more than 60 miles distant, and weekenders. There is no economic reason for the village shop, the pub or even a spiritual reason for the church. All have gone; to be converted to yet another 'desirable country residence'.

This Suffolk Chronicle charts the changes as they occurred in a West Suffolk village between 1969 and 1994. In this case the village still lives, with its shop, two of its pubs, its church and two chapels, and a school. The source of the Chronicle is the 'Wickhambrook Scene', a bi-monthly magazine produced by the Wickhambrook Community Association and edited by the author for 18 of those years. In 1994 it was the Suffolk runner-up in a competition for village magazines organised by the British Association of Industrial Editors.

In many instances intriguing flashbacks are also given of Suffolk village life between the wars, and even back to the turn of the century, in the words of Wickhambrook villagers in their letters and reports to 'The Scene'. Additionally, through personal reminiscences and the results of readers' own researches, the rich history of the area stretching back to Saxon times, appears as a second strand in this Suffolk Chronicle.

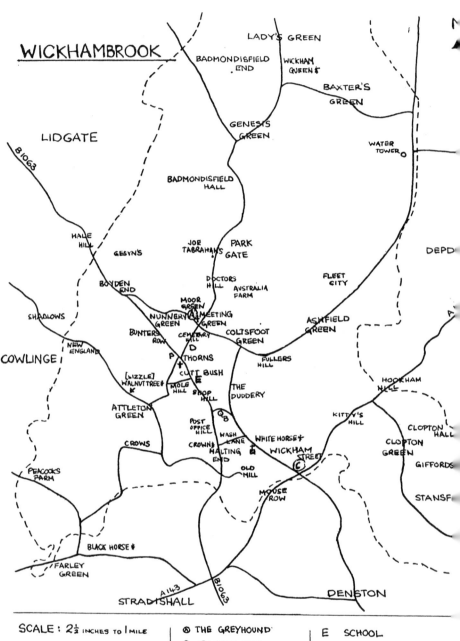

WICKHAMBROOK

LADY'S GREEN
BADMONDISFIELD END
WICKHAM QUEEN'S
BAXTER'S GREEN

LIDGATE

GENESIS GREEN

WATER TOWER

BADMONDISFIELD HALL

B1063

HALE HILL
GESYN'S
JOE TABRAHAM'S
PARK GATE
DEPD

BOYDEN END
DOCTORS HILL
AUSTRALIA FARM
FLEET CITY

SHADLOWS
MOOR GREEN
NUNNERY GREEN
MEETING GREEN
ASHFIELD GREEN

COWLINGE
NEW ENGLAND
BUNTERS ROW
CEMETERY HILL
COLTSFOOT GREEN
FULLERS HILL
HOOKHAM HILL

D THORNS
P
CUTT BUSH

[LIZZLE] WALNUT TREE
MOLE HILL
SHOP HILL
THE DUDDERY
KITTY'S HILL
CLOPTON HALL

ATTLETON GREEN
POST OFFICE HILL
Q B
CLOPTON GREEN

CROWS
WASH LANE
WHITE HORSE
GIFFORDS

CROWN HALTING END
WICKHAM STREET
C

PEACOCKS FARM
OLD MILL
STANSF

MOUSE ROW

BLACK HORSE

FARLEY GREEN

A143
STRADISHALL
B1063
DENSTON

SCALE: 2½ INCHES TO 1 MILE

ROADS
PARISH BOUNDARY
ALL SAINTS CHURCH
CHAPELS

Ⓐ THE GREYHOUND
Q B CLOAK INN
Ⓒ THE PLUMBER'S ARMS
P POST OFFICE

E SCHOOL
✠ OLD PUBLIC HOUSES
D WICKHAMBROOK MEMORIAL SOCIAL CENTRE AND RECREATION GROUND

Introduction

It was a Monday morning in early March 1973. Following the departure of the removal van early Saturday afternoon, my wife and I spent the rest of the day making some semblance of order on the groundfloor of our cottage. Sunday, we dismantled the bed and took the back off the wardrobe and knocked out one side in order that we could get them both up the narrow staircase that wound back on itself. Both were then reassembled with passable success, although it is doubtful if approval would have been given by a competent carpenter. 'Any bedroom furniture in 1590 must have been much simpler to get up *those* stairs', said Marion.

With the exertions of the weekend's furniture arranging behind us, I had strolled into the garden, with a cup of coffee and a panatella, to savour the first signs of spring in our new country home.

'Morning Guv! GPO flying squad here!'

I turned round from admiring the attempts of the first daffodils to break through the weeds of an overgrown flower bed to see a wiry individual in his late fifties riding a bike of some vintage up my garden path. It had a luggage rack on the back, upon which, tied up with string, was a pile of letters. He had a GPO badge attached to the lapel of his jacket, which bore little resemblance to a conventional postman's uniform.

This was our first introduction to a Wickhambrook resident: Fred Thearle, the village postman for some ten years. And it was not without significance that Fred and his wife Maggie were not Wickhambrook born, or even East Anglian, but had moved from Battersea, South London, some four years before.

Fred is blessed with a great cockney sense of humour, which no doubt kept him going during two years as a prisoner of war in Germany, following capture in the Italian campaign. This enabled him to become eventually accepted by even the most dour of Wickhambrook's Suffolk residents as he made his way round the village each day with the mail.

Following his retirement, he and his wife were members of the Wickhambrook Community Council Committee for several years during the late seventies and early eighties, also collating the pages of the bi-monthly 'Wickhambrook Scene' in their front room.

In addition, Fred and I used to run off the editorial pages on an ancient duplicator which was stored in a small room at the back of the stage in our village Memorial Hall. I forget now who started out helping whom, but both of us were invariably covered in duplicating ink before half the job was done. The fact that we used to hold conversations in ungrammatical pidgeon German probably did little for our concentration.

'Herr Bean, die machine ist gebuggered'.

When we first started, one of the small windows had a hole in it, which we blocked up with a piece of cardboard to keep out the East Anglian winter wind. Later, as 'genteel' vandalism first spread to Wickhambrook, several panes of glass became broken, with the result that our duplicating paper was invariably damp, causing numerous production problems.

■

I have always loved mountains and used to have the occasional daydream of moving to Scotland, where I could continue my technical writing. In consequence, I sometimes wonder how I came to live in gently undulating West Suffolk.

According to the address on the envelopes that came through our door we used to live in Surrey. In reality, Thornton Heath 'Surrey' was an extension of London with the nearest green field being some four miles away. I had accepted this as part of life, and for my own particular occupation it seemed that to live within the London area was the logical thing to do. As no doubt many young people born in villages or country towns may feel, when you are under thirty the life of the big city certainly has its attractions. It is where 'everything happens', you believe, although on reflection I am not so sure. Then you begin to question the purpose of all the 'hustle and bustle'. For the successful, it might bring the reward of material things, but for me it did not bring any true feeling of the purpose of life as God or Nature intended.

I feel that the reason for this is that although man can live with contentment in a market town or even in a natural city like Norwich or Cambridge, he/she was not intended to live in such a large expanse of brick, concrete and tarmac as London is today. It is a place to work, a place to visit for the arts, the shops, the sporting events. But it is not a place to 'live' in the full sense of the word.

With its teeming population and now a variety of immigrant groups, who seem not to have heard of the 'multiracial society' concept and in the main want little to do with anybody outside their own particular cultural group, one somehow never has the inclination to get to know anybody outside a close circle of friends. In contrast, in two years in Wickhambrook we got to know far more people than after living in the same South London house for 17 years.

For these reasons, mainly of frustration, we decided that I could still make some sort of living without the need to live in London. A country area within striking distance of London was our objective: but where? Three or four times a year over a period of four years we started visiting friends who had left the outer South London area to start life anew some eight miles east of Bury St Edmunds. Thus began our contact with Suffolk.

At first we hoped that the weather would be fine for each impending visit. Then we began to realise that the weather made little effect on our enjoyment. This is surely the test for a 'towny' deciding whether or not to live in the country. It does not mean tripping through cowslip glades with the sun shining through the trees as in a TV commercial for hair lacquer, but squelching over muddy footpaths in your wellies with cold rain driving into your face yet still enjoying your surroundings.

Unlike Surrey, Kent or the southern part of Essex, we found that Suffolk was far less influenced by the great wen, even though here it is only 60 miles away. When we came there was still a strong sense of unity among the people, with a consequent definite Suffolk character. Sadly, this has become somewhat weakened over twenty years. Perhaps one of the reasons for this retention of the Suffolk character is that with its numerous old cottages, houses, halls and churches, Suffolk is constantly reminded of its past – and with no identifiable past there is often no future.

Thus we escaped from London and came to West Suffolk, and via the house Ads in the *Bury Free Press*, to Wickhambrook.

Like many other 'immigrants' who came to Suffolk by choice, we soon became rather selfish. We felt resentful of too many more people coming into *our* village, whether from London, Birmingham, or the other Midlands towns and cities. This affliction was an early touch of NIMBYism (Not In My Backyard) from which many of us now suffer.

Although only a cottage, our home itself is modestly interesting, both architecturally and historically. Part of a larger building, it was built about 1590 of timber frame and wattle and daub construction with inglenook fireplaces and a thatched roof. Yes, the roses are near, but not round, the door.

Rumour has it that the heart of oak beams used in the construction were once destined for Queen Elizabeth's ships that were hastily being built in 1588 to defeat the Spanish Armada, but due to Drake's fire ships and bad weather, became surplus to requirements. It is a fact that in East Anglia as a whole there are a large number of surviving timber framed buildings of that period.

Until midway through the 19th century the building as a whole was the Wickhambrook Workhouse and has often been referred to by contributors to the 'Wickhambrook Scene'. Needless to say, 'Christmas Day in the Workhouse' is still invariably 'full of fun'.

Wickhambrook is often described as being 'ten miles from anywhere'. It is in fact ten miles from Bury St Edmunds, nine and a half miles from Newmarket and eight miles from Haverhill. The Cambridgeshire border is but six miles away at its nearest point and North

9

Essex some ten miles. The nearest M11 junction, whose completion accelerated population changes in the village, is under 30 minutes drive away.

The village is made up of eleven quite separate greens and covers an area of nearly twenty square miles. Thus, with a population of little more than 1100, including children, it is the largest in area in Suffolk.

Of the several halls in Wickhambrook – Giffords, Clopton, Butlers, Gaines, and Badmondisfield, it is the latter that is most interesting historically. The manor of Badmondisfield derives its name from an early Saxon possessor. It was held in the reign of Edward the Confessor by the Earl Algar. Because of the rebellion of his sons, Edwin and Morcar, against William the Conqueror it passed to the crown. Badmondisfield is mentioned in the Domesday Book.

Neighbouring villages, which are often referred to by contributors to 'The Scene', include Cowlinge, Lidgate, Ousden, Hargrave, Depden, Denston, Stradishall and Stansfield. Some older residents still say that he or she is not really local for 'she were born in Lidgate', or one of the other villages.

As in Wickhambrook, it was not until after the Second World War that many of the side roads in the area received a permanent hard surfacing. Electricity for all did not arrive until 1953 and mains sewage not until 1970. Indeed, some areas are still on septic tanks.

Until 1983 Wickhambrook was in the safe Tory Parliamentary Constituency of Bury St Edmunds and was represented for many years by Sir Eldon Griffiths. Boundary changes as a result of Suffolk's expanding population meant that Wickhambrook was transferred to the new seat of Suffolk South, with a new MP, one Mr Tim Yeo.

Disapproval of his love life by the strong non-conformist element to be found in Suffolk – and who historically have tended to be liberal supporters – could mean that Tim Yeo's 17,000 majority could be overturned by the Liberal Democrats at the next election. On the other hand, it has yet to be seen how strong is the support for the opinion expressed by one Wickhambrook local:

'Seems the old boy did his job. He jist got caught out doing what a lot of other folk do git up to.'

With the advent of the National Health Service in 1945 Wickhambrook-based GPs covered the day-to-day medical requirements for this general area. Until 1980, their surgery, perhaps limited in comparison with today's high standards, was based at the home of Dr John Batt, whose father had practised there before him. Known as the White House, until the mid-twenties it was a pub called the White Horse. The medical services, based on a personal knowledge of so many of the patients, offered by Dr Batt and his partner Dr Philip Forsythe is legendary among many older people.

Following the retirement of Dr Forsythe, Dr Batt (also now

retired) and new colleagues in partnership opened up a purpose-built surgery at Nunnery Green in 1980. Today, this surgery must be the envy of many doctors' partnerships in our towns and cities.

Over the past thirty years Wickhambrook has seen a number of entertainment world celebrities take up residence in the area for a time, and not all as weekenders. These have included Jane Asher – with Paul McCartney as a frequent visitor, Diane Soloman the country and western singer, and Jenny Seagrove, whose former husband, the Indian born actor Madhav Sharma, still stays in residence and can sometimes be met in the best local watering holes.

However, this Chronicle has much more to do with the ordinary people, farming folk and country life in general than the world of entertainment.

■

It was in the evening of that same Monday in March 1973 when we had first met Fred Thearle that we came across 'The Cloak'.

Strangely enough it was Marion and not I who had first suggested that we should look to see if there was a village pub.

'On Saturday I thought I saw a pub sign down that lane right of the dip in the road before you come up to the shop,' she said.

As it was then dark, we got into our Mark 1 Cortina and drove the three-quarters of a mile to where we thought the pub stood.

'This is not a pub, it's more like a Methodist Chapel,' I said, gazing at a dimly lit building. We could hear the rise and fall of three or four country voices from inside and an irregular clicking noise. We opened the door nearest to the source of the noise, which was in fact the public bar. The door alongside opened into the saloon bar which we were later to find looked like somebody's drawing room from the 1930s and was seldom used.

In the public bar that night sat four gents playing dominoes and another person sitting at one corner of the bar by himself. The players included the late Billy Underwood, Norton Hicks and Jack Mortlock, the landlord, and the only one to look up as we came in.

'Good evening', he said, 'are you visitors to our village or newcomers?'

Having deprived us of 13p for two halves of bitter, he quickly made us welcome, with a smile and a joke or two, so much so that I was persuaded to stay for another – or two.

Thus began our introduction to Wickhambrook and our friendship with Jack Mortlock, one of the world's characters and gentlemen. He was a founder member of the Wickhambrook Community Council Committee and, particularly in the early days, a regular contributor of droll articles to 'The Scene'.

Jack was born at Pump Cottage, Coltsfoot Green, Wickhambrook in 1915, one of seven children. He obtained a scholarship to Haverhill School, cycling the eight miles each way at the age of 11 years. At the age of 14 years and nine months he enlisted in the RAOC at Bury St Edmunds and trained as an armourer in Portsmouth where he was later to meet his wife, his companion for some 32 years until her untimely death in 1969.

Jack travelled extensively with the Army and between 1936 and 1962 visited more than 40 countries without being stationed in Europe or east of Iraq. He was at this time arguably the most travelled soldier in the British Army.

During his travels he was to meet the rich and famous, including the Aga Khan, the Duke of Windsor, Errol Flynn, Robert Mitchum, Rita Hayworth and some unsavoury individuals such as Lucky Luciano in Miami. Whilst working as a 'Diplomatic Courier' for British Intelligence, liaising with his case officer Ian Fleming of James Bond fame and the Washington connection 'Intrepid', he told me he was obliged to associate with Nazi low life in South American 'dives'.

Throughout his travels he never forgot his rural roots and his desire to return to Wickhambrook. At the age of 54 he retired from the Army as a Warrant Officer and became landlord of The Cloak public house. He was mine host for some ten enjoyable years, making more friends and welcoming newcomers to the village. When he finally retired from The Cloak he remained a regular with his own seat at one corner of the bar and a source of 'advice' to new landlords until the pub's untimely close in 1989.

One of Jack's brothers, Victor Mortlock, died in tragic circumstances during the war. Captured at Singapore, he and several hundred other British prisoners were crammed into a Japanese cargo ship to be taken to Japan to work as slave labourers. The ship was torpedoed by an American submarine, who were not to know who was on board, and went down leaving no survivors.

Another brother, Arthur, was killed in a road accident in the village in 1976.

Being a widower from 1969 was no doubt one of the reasons why The Cloak in his day would almost certainly fall foul of today's Health & Safety regulations. The gentleman's urinal, for example, was across the yard and open to the heavens. One often stood there with feet crunching autumn leaves, even if it was the following May, or June.

In winter months there would be a smouldering, rather than roaring, log fire, in front of which was an old tattered carpet. This was frequently possessed by two old mongrel dogs, one of them Jack's, who would slumber away, with the occasional growl or breaking of wind, amongst the remnants of a few well chewed chop bones.

Nevertheless, The Cloak had a special ambience for its more dedicated regulars, which they could not find at that time in the other two village pubs, the Greyhound and the Plumbers Arms.

At closing time – or perhaps a little after, Jack would say: 'When

I finally call time I want gentlemen out of that door and ladies up those stairs.'

Rumour has it that in spite of his ill-fitting wig he had an occasional acceptance.

Jack Mortlock died suddenly in July 1992. Some thought that if his beloved Cloak was still open he would have been encouraged to walk there every evening, instead of becoming a semi-recluse, which would have prolonged his life.

Two of his three sons, Chris and Peter, with their wives, still live in the village and keep their father's Mortlock sense of humour alive. I am indebted to Chris for some of the background information on his father.

From the point of view of this Chronicle his articles for 'The Scene' reflected his interest in local history, farming lore and the Suffolk dialect which he managed to lose during the course of his 40 years odyssey.

■

When Jack left The Cloak in 1975 there was a succession of six different landlords and their wives until Greene King the brewers decided to close it. Apparently, like so many country pubs, it was no longer profitable enough.

The first new tenant had been a former paint chemist, who had spent many years in Malaysia. He knocked the two bars into one, installed new loos, exposed more beams and took the pub from the thirties to the seventies without diminishing its character. He had aspirations as a master chef and modern pub grub arrived in Wickhambrook. Due to his and his much younger wife's predilections for the bottle there were times when what you received did not quite match up to what you ordered. Nevertheless, the jolly couple, as with most of their successors, ensured that The Cloak became the choice of venue for couples out for the evening, various 'characters' of the village and surrounding area, and later the Cricket Club.

Many an eventful Christmas Eve and New Year's Party was held there, particularly with the last couple to hold the sacred office, Dick and Angie from Cambridge.

Well spoken Landlady Angie would frequently inquire of her *regular* male customers: 'How's your Willie?'

This did not indicate a loose moral character on her part, but a natural sense of the ridiculous, if not outrageous.

Dick, quietly spoken and always impeccably dressed, would see to his customers' wants, whilst smiling gently at his wife's more extrovert comments. Only the expert observer could detect that by the end of an evening Dick had often quietly put away as much as his best customers.

I have mentioned earlier that one of the four men playing dominoes in The Cloak on that night of our first visit was Bill Underwood. The 'person sitting at one corner of the bar by himself' was Bill Wright.

Billy Underwood was a 'foreigner'. Born in Stansfield, some four miles away, he came to Wickhambrook in 1927 to work at Justin Brooke's fruit farm, then quite intensive in labour employment. The concept of a village hall as a war memorial was said to be his idea and he was elected to the committee at the first meeting of the Village Hall Committee in January 1945.

He was an early active member of the Wickhambrook Football Club and in later life one of its most dedicated, and vocal, supporters. In fact, some said that the manner of his support, even when in his seventies, bordered on football hooliganism.

In 1977 Greene King's PR department decided that an evening 'do' should be put on in The Cloak to mark Billy Underwood's 50 years of custom. 'Only times I not been here John', he told me, 'was when I been ill.'

This was not strictly true, as he was also a regular visitor at one time to The Greyhound.

With the local press in attendance, Greene King's PR lady asked Billy if he had always drunk their IPA bitter or did he prefer their Abbott's Ale.

'Oh no, I don't like any o' that stuff,' he said, his blue eyes twinkling: 'I just drink Guinness!' Greene King were not amused. Billy Underwood died some three years later.

Bill Wright used to occupy his own regular seat at the corner of the bar in The Cloak. In latter years Jack Mortlock would occupy the opposite corner stool (someone compared them to two bookends), but the two found there was too big a mental gap between them for any meaningful conversation, particularly when Bill Wright had had a skinful.

'That Jack Mortlock don't know nuffen,' Bill would say.

Born and bred in the village, Bill also worked for Justin Brooke's for many years prior to his retirement. Although there were more than a few occasions when he was incapable of riding his bike home from the pub at closing time, the following morning you would see him riding off to work on time – if *you* were up early enough.

Today you can find Bill, sometimes a little more cantankerous, in a corner of the bar in The Greyhound.

Justin Brooke and his wife Edith came to Wickhambrook from Devon just after the First World War. Purchasing several hundred acres of farmland they soon became West Suffolk's leading producers of soft fruit and apples. To this was added a dairy herd, a dairy and a milk delivery service that went as far as the city of Cambridge. With the recession of the Thirties there were many families in Wickhambrook, Denston, Stradishall and other villages that were grateful for the work he provided.

They were great ones for strange nicknames in Wickhambrook

throughout most of this century and earlier. Bill Wright's for some reason was 'Shacker'. Others are still often referred to by their nicknames. To give a few examples, there is 'Smokes', who has never smoked; 'The Rat', now running a successful small engineering business; 'The Snake', who is most un-snakelike in character but a genius in motor repairs; and 'Phoebe', a barrel-chested, good humoured Greyhound regular, far removed from a Greek Goddess. To my knowledge, few under 40 seem to have any of these odd nicknames.

■

With the closing of The Cloak in 1989, after being a pub for some 200 years, the regulars wandered around the area like lost souls looking for a replacement. But there was not to be a real replacement: The Cloak was a part of Wickhambrook life that has also gone.

The Greyhound is another long established pub and until 1974 was run for many years by Ted Hicks and his wife. The Hicks's are a prominent family in Wickhambrook and the surrounding villages, with roots going back many generations. Its atmosphere in the sixties and early seventies are epitomised by the wording of its advertisement in the early issues of 'The Scene'.

'The Greyhound – the friendly pub. Call in for a chat and
a quiet drink.'

At least ninety per cent of the customers in those days were local born people. Once they got to know you they were certainly a friendly crowd, young and old. At weekends in particular it would be buzzing with Suffolk dialect and laughter. Among them were peasant faces which had stepped straight out of Peter Bruegel's painting, 'The Wedding Feast'. Today, The Greyhound is run by a lively and cheerful London landlady, Gill Gosling.

With the passage of twenty years, the old Suffolk accent is hardly heard, except from a handful of the older locals who are still customers. With its live bands, Karaoke nights and disco music, at weekends it is now very much a young people's pub. Their talk is the universal youth-speak of nineties Britain with its blurred pastiche of cultural and geographical backgrounds. On a Saturday night you could almost be in West Ham or West Bromwich rather than Wickhambrook, although you would undoubtedly be a lot safer. Not all the Cockney voices you hear will be those of people born within ten miles, let alone the sound of, Bow Bells. Some of the girls and young men were born in Suffolk but, in the manner of Nigel Kennedy, have adopted 'Estuary English', the hybrid London working class accent, as the fashionable thing to do.

Strictly speaking The Plumbers Arms is in Denston, some 50 yards over the Wickhambrook border. Situated on the main Haverhill to Bury St Edmunds road, it also has a long history.

Until the arrival of the present landlord and landlady, Jim and

Marilyn Pruden (both East Anglian) some twelve years ago, there was little to distinguish The Plumbers Arms from any other West Suffolk pub. The decor was and still is rather basic.

Jim and Marilyn, as well as daughter and son, are regular worshippers at Wickhambrook All Saints Church and have a wide taste in music, with a preference for the melodious classical and trad jazz. Their combined interests and knowledge are also far-ranging, which makes a change for those customers who may want to talk about something other than who is going to win the 3.30 at Newmarket or whose husband is sleeping with whose wife.

Perhaps not surprisingly, The Plumbers Arms have always fielded a strong quiz team in the local Greene King league since they became a feature of modern pub life. In 1993 they were the runners-up in the grand final covering Greene King's pubs stretching from London to Norwich, from Ipswich to Bedford. Landlady Marilyn was a member of that successful team.

No 'afters' are served in 'The Plumbers', which means that it has attracted many of the early drinkers, now known as members of the '5 O'clock Club'. From 5.30 until around 8.00 pm every week day and Saturday, a diverse assortment of personalities, predominantly male, assemble to talk, to banter, some to play pool and nearly all to drink beer. 'Members' include a farm worker; a farmer; a freelance TV programme producer; a senior probation officer; a factory worker; a bank manager; a PR executive; two senior lady nurses; a builder; a psychiatrist; two prison officers from nearby Highpoint Prison; a couple of sales managers; a deep sea diver, when on leave; a hair dresser for the film industry, when not on location; a TV video editor (mainly 'resting'), the proprietor of a flower stall, and a wartime member of the SOE who holds the Military Cross. A number are former regulars of The Cloak.

Whilst the majority of 'members' are non-Suffolk in origin, it is interesting to note that almost all have lived in the area for at least ten years.

Usually by 8.00 pm most 5 O'clock Club members would have departed for home, with only one or two new customers appearing until 9.30, when the 'second shift' of regulars would appear: nearly all living in close proximity to the pub and nearly all Suffolk born.

The exception to the eight o'clock exodus would be a birthday celebration or the like, when certain club members would produce guitars, mandolins, mouth organs, etc. for an evening session. Joined by wives and girl friends, the music would be a combination of folk music and renditions of the classic pops. The 5 O'clock Club Members Band will often be joined by Landlord Jim on guitar and daughter Claire on clarinet, saxophone or whatever wind instrument is to hand.

Readers can be forgiven for thinking that so far this introduction to the Wickhambrook Chronicle is an anthology of village pub life, past and present. However, the point is that the role of the pub in a living village has far more importance as a meeting place than does a city pub. The other major meeting places are the churches and chapels and the village shop. An extra bonus in Wickhambrook for young people is that there is now a well-organised and well-attended youth club; in this case a change for the better.

■

Like most of East Anglia, Wickhambrook has a strong Methodist and Non-Conformist and therefore teetotal tradition. Prior to the sixties local people in general either met in the Methodist Chapel or Congregational Church or one of the pubs, seldom both. Only the Church of England's followers and the few Catholics could combine the use of both meeting places.

Today, when we have more Moslems than Methodists in Britain, fewer young people are attending the local chapel and churches with their parents. If they have outgrown the youth club they are more likely to be found slipping into The Greyhound to meet their peers. 'Don't tell my Dad you saw me here', they say.

An upholder of the old non-conformist way of life is the much respected Alfred Hicks, brother of the former landlord of The Greyhound. Known as 'Mr Wickhambrook' because of his active participation in so many of the village's organisations, octagenarian Alf Hicks was a lay preacher and Sunday School teacher at the Congregational Chapel (now United Reformed Church), for many years.

Born in the village he attended Wickhambrook School (which is still open) and shared a desk with his wife-to-be, Ivy. Sadly she died some ten years ago.

He has been a correspondent to the *Bury Free Press* for 50 years, charting the changes of the village. He is still the most prolific contributor to 'The Scene', with regular reports on the Horticultural Society, Wickhambrook History Society, Snooker Club, Over Sixties Club, the Boys Brigade, of which he has been an officer for 50 years, general village events plus, of course, the United Reformed Church.

A founder member of the Wickhambrook Community Council in 1967 (now Community Association), he attended that first public meeting in 1945 to discuss the building of a village Memorial Hall.

Alf Hicks was also an elected member of the Wickhambrook Parish Council for 35 years, in the days when all seven councillors were truly local people. In 1994 only three are.

The chairman for nearly 20 years is Peter Bayman, a usually jovial John Bull type farmer, but with a short fuse, who came from Essex in 1956.

He was another founder member of the Wickhambrook Community Council and was the Secretary for more than fifteen years. During that time he has been the driving force behind the village annual carnival, held in conjunction with the flower show, and Wick-hambrook's bonfire night which almost became his personal fiefdom.

Pantomimes, Carol Concerts, Old Time Music Hall nights, have all become regular events at the village Memorial Hall over the past decade, at which the lighting effects in particular have been praise-worthy features. The man in charge of these is again Peter Bayman and, as with the fireworks, no small amount has been paid for out of his own pocket.

There are many who have incurred Peter's wrath, only to be greeted with a smile twenty minutes later. Following a recent mild heart attack, which was perhaps no surprise, he has developed the art of counting up to ten.

Another farmer on the Parish Council is Jeff Claydon, also active in the development of the village's six acres of sports facilities. The Claydons have farmed in Wickhambrook since Jeff's great-grandfather's days, when it was, of course, labour intensive. Today, he and his brother Frank run the whole farm by themselves.

As elsewhere in the area, crops are primarily barley, wheat, rape-seed and beans. The clay soil in the immediate vicinity is too heavy for sugar beet or other root crops. However one or two venturesome souls have added a touch of colour, other than rapeseed yellow, with the blue of linseed and golden sunflowers.

The only farm animals to be seen in the whole area, apart from horses, are a few sheep and pigs. Our near neighbours Julian and Anne Wilson raise some lambs for the early market and do 'bed and breakfast' for racehorses in transit.

Many smaller fields have been combined since the war to accommo-date the larger farm machinery, particularly combine harvesters. Compared with Cambridgeshire and Mid-Suffolk however, our countryside still has a look of England and not a North American prairie.

Frank Claydon has an obsessional hobby. He loves to fly his micro-light. As he is joined from time to time by one or two fellow enthusi-asts flying off the Claydon's land it was understandable that some opposition arose within the village, although a petition for and against revealed it was in a minority. Surprisingly for those who think that farmers always stand together, one of the opposition leaders was Peter Bayman. One wag suggested that this was because his wife did not want to be overlooked when sunbathing topless in the garden. However, Frank Claydon, who lost an eye in an accident as a boy, said he would only look with his glass eye as he needed the good one to watch the controls and navigate.

■

I recall being told by one of the local Parish Councillors, Vic Harrod (who until his death was the longest serving Councillor), that when you had lived in the village twenty-one years you could apply for a

West Suffolk passport. 'Whether you do get it is a different matter', he added.

The proprietors of the village shop can make their application.

Jim Mayes and his wife came to Wickhambrook in 1972 after running a shop in a Surrey village. Now managed by daughter Barbara, it is also a post office and a petrol station. It manages to survive as most villagers realise that you don't have to have an A level in Economics to see that a trip to the nearest supermarket means an expenditure of at least £3 on petrol and wear and tear of your car before you purchase anything. You could go by bus, but only to Bury St Edmunds and only once a day or twice on market days.

Recent letters in 'The Scene' regarding the future of the shop, as also the pubs, extol readers to 'use it or lose it'. Until three years ago the nearest other village shop was at Cowlinge, some two and a half miles away. Run by Trevor Foreman, a local-born middle-aged bachelor, it was a nineteen-forties time-warp. It is doubtful if Trevor had ever heard of 'sell-by dates'. Apart from such fast-moving items as butter, marge, bacon, sugar, eggs, etc., many other items were still marked in pounds, shillings and old pence. People swear that there were some items that went back to before the war. No, Trevor did not like to throw things away.

If the outside leaves on a lettuce or a cabbage had gone a bit yellow, Trevor would pull them off to reveal a certain inner greenness which could be offered to you for half-price. If he knew you were a bit hard-up, you could have it for nothing. Trevor was that sort of person. Sadly he died three years ago, a victim of cancer.

Amongst the 'newcomers' to Wickhambrook who have long received their West Suffolk passports are various foreigners such as Scots, Brummies and a couple of Geordies. There are even two whose original homelands were across the seas.

In 1945 an Italian prisoner of war, Giuseppe Di-Giulio, was released from captivity. He decided not to go home, for he had fallen in love with a Wickhambrook girl. 'Joe the Italian' soon found himself some work: trundling a wheelbarrow full of stones he filled in the pot-holes of the side roads and lanes under contract for the Council. By dint of sheer hard work over many years he was able to purchase several acres of rich Fen soil at West Row, some fifteen miles away, ideal for vegetable growing.

Joe is probably the only person who speaks English with a mix of Italian and broad Suffolk accents. As he stands outside his house, aptly named Joelanda, selling his vegetables on a Sunday morning, you might hear him say: 'I go to hella boya! You eata they taters already!'

In 1946 a young German girl walked into The Cloak – probably the first German ever to do so. This was Marie, who had come over to England from the ruins of Rostock to find work. Although they hardly understood a word of each other's language, that night she met Les Hurrell, who was to become her husband.

Les, whose family have been in the village for several generations, had spent much of the war at sea in the Royal Navy. This included, at the age of 19, the highly dangerous job of escorting Arctic convoys to Russia while being repeatedly dive-bombed and under threat from U-Boats.

Marie found that being German there were some who would not speak to her at first, which was not unusual immediately after the war. This was not the case with Les Hurrell, as with most of the men who actually saw action, and in a short time they were married and happily so until 1989 when Les tragically died of a heart attack. Widow Marie did not go back to Germany, but remains to this day amongst her many friends in Wickhambrook.

Not yet eligible for his 'passport', as he has only lived in the village for eight or nine years, is Manuel, a Spanish psychiatrist who works for the local health authority. Married to an English girl and father of three sons, Manuel is also a visitor from time to time to the 'Five O'clock Club'. And like most Mediterraneans, you may see him merry, but never drunk!

Returning to the contributors to 'The Scene', past and present, not all have been without their critics. One such contributor was the late Stanley Golding.

He would spend hours going through various church records and also spent much time at Bury St Edmunds Records Office. Usually this would be in his role as an amateur genealogist trying to sort out somebody's family tree. Sometimes at the same time he would prepare a page headed 'Other Days' for 'The Scene'. Unfortunately Stanley Golding's researches were often obsessed with the subjects of incest and interference with young girls. When told he should mix it with other recorded happenings of the time to give a more balanced report, his answer would be: 'That is what a lot of people got up to in those days.'

Here are just three examples out of seven similar ones making up an article of his that I refused to publish in its entirety in 'The Scene'. There is little wonder that many women in Wickhambrook thought he was the epitome of a 'dirty old man'.

Workhouse Accounts, Wickhambrook
1788 James Taylor to have the girl Parker out of the Workhouse at 1s per week and to leave the girl as desent as he find her.
1789 Joseph Button to take out of the Parish Sarah Simmonds from Easter 1789–Easter 1790 at 1s per week and find her in desent clothing and leave her as he find her.

Dalham (a village four miles from Wickhambrook)
1686   Baptised: Elizabeth, ye base child of James Taylor and
Mary Taylor who were brother and sister.

Irrespective of whether or not Stanley was a dirty old man, he was certainly an intelligent one, an interesting one and a controversial one. He was an Army bandsman in the First World War and a musician for several hotel 'Palm Court' orchestras between the wars. He came to Suffolk in 1950 and moved into a lonely cottage between Wickhambrook and Cowlinge around 1956, where he stayed until his death at the end of 1988, aged 91.

He was without running water or electricity and up until his 75th year he would often take a bath by climbing into his water butt. For that reason I made a point of not taking water with my whisky when invited to accept Stanley's hospitality. On such occasions he would often decide to play the piano; some Chopin or a military march, the music for which he read without glasses until into his eighties.

He had strong views on the Church of England and deplored all of its modernist trends, from the dropping of the King James' bible to the inauguration of women priests. Often he would draw a stinging reply in 'The Scene' from our local vicar and was even able to get the local bishop to rush into print. Despite his devout Christian beliefs, I recall Stanley replying to my question 'Who do you think was the greatest European since Charlemagne?' 'Either Napoleon or Hitler,' he replied. But that was Stanley, probably being outrageous.

Up until the end, Stanley would drink half a bottle of Scotch a day at his home, plus two or three Strong Suffolk ales with his lunch at The Cloak and smoked thirty fags a day. In his later years he was best to be avoided as he drove home from his lunchtime trip in his DAF car at 15 mph.

Stanley had had quite a full love-life, apparently having been married three times and lived with two women.

His youngest daughter, who would visit him from time to time, had similar appetites to her father. A heavy drinker and smoker, intelligent, and a good conversationalist when not too drunk, she dispensed her pleasures to several local males in Wickhambrook's cornfields in addition to, it is said, a passing peer of the realm. She died of cancer at the age of 39, one year before her father's death.

In the extracts from 'The Scene' that follows there are several contributions in the last decade from Colin Bird, who took over as village postman when Fred Thearle retired. Now some fifteen years in the village, Colin has taken up the cudgels with enthusiasm for a number of causes; most to the village's advantage. He is also on the Parish Council and at one time was chairman of the Community Association, until his restless energies set him off on another task. His

21

acerbic wit comes through in his reports, particularly when writing as 'Messenger'.

Then there was 'Barfly', whose tongue-in-cheek comments used to provide irritation, amusement or boredom, in equal amounts, among 'Scene' readers. He did not start writing until 1986 and it is doubtful if editors in the early days would have accepted his initial esoteric accounts of Five O'clock Club 'low life'. In later issues he widened the horizons of his 'View From a Bar Stool' by extending them into the wider world of Wickhambrook and even beyond.

'Barfly' was Bernard Young, an Assistant Governor at Highpoint Prison who took up residence with his wife and three teenage children in the village in 1984. Extremely knowledgeable on a wide range of subjects, he was the backbone of one of the Plumbers Arms quiz teams. Composed of prison officers, it was known as the 'Plumbers Mates'.

Possibly because of being continuously passed over for promotion, Bernard the Barfly became a heavy drinker. As he spread his custom amongst some half-a-dozen pubs in the area, few realised how much he did drink and such was his capacity that fewer ever saw him drunk. The nearest I got to it was when he delivered his copy for 'The Scene' to my house at 10.45 one winter's evening and fell over a flower tub.

'J.B. do you realise I could sue you', he said, with blood dripping on to his shoe. But he never did

Poor Barfly literally died of the drink. Having spent two months in Addenbrookes Hospital, Cambridge, in 1993 fighting for his life, he died on the operating table whilst undergoing his third liver transplant.

His funeral at All Saints Church, Wickhambrook, was attended by three landlords and three landladies, amongst family and many people from the village. His forty-strong guard of honour, composed of former prison officer colleagues, which lined the path from the church door to the hearse, was soaked to the skin by a sudden cloud burst as the coffin came forth. Barfly's sense of humour did not fail him, even in the end.

Highpoint Prison, less than a mile outside Wickhambrook's boundaries, was formerly RAF Stradishall, adjacent to the village of Stradishall. It utilises many of the original buildings which have been converted to prison use.

As an airbase it was operative from 1938 to 1970. During that period it was at different times a fighter, bomber, transport and training establishment. In the total time it was operative, 640 young men lost their lives flying from there with a loss of 140 aircraft of all types. Although most of the losses were, as to be expected, during the war, a significant number were from the critical post-war years when young men flew and trained hard before moving to fighter squadrons.

The site is on the second highest point in Suffolk, 420 feet above sea level and anyone flying due east from there would not pass over higher ground until reaching the Ural mountains. This goes a long way in explaining why it gets so cold when the winter wind is coming out of the east!

During the war RAF Stradishall was a major base for Wellington and then Stirling bombers and was in the forefront of the hard-fought bomber offensive over Germany.

What is less well known and in fact has only been divulged in recent years, is that it was a major base from which gallant SOE agents, female as well as male, were flown into German occupied Europe. The aircraft used were mainly Westland Lysanders with some Whitley's. A former pilot told us that his job was really like a taxi-driver. Any Germans lying in wait were not interested in him: only the agents they were delivering or picking up.

An NCO engineer from Tyneside who was based at Stradishall during the war was Ron Penhaligan. He stayed on in Wickhambrook after the war, having married the local baker's daughter. The business, Rowling & Cooke, is still going strong with fresh baked bread (with no additives) being delivered to your door by the grand-children of Mr and Mrs Penhaligan.

After its closure in 1970 the camp buildings stood empty for a couple of years. Then on the international scene came the expulsion of Uganda's Asian community by Idi Amin.

For some reason, which I have never fully understood, they did not return to India or Pakistan, but came to Britain. Many of them came via the former RAF Stradishall, which had been turned into a transit camp for them. There is no record of any settling permanently in West Suffolk.

Since the opening of the former RAF base as a prison for Category C prisoners (non-violent) it has achieved the record of having the highest number of escapees of any UK prison. One week in 1992 thirteen 'went over the wall'.

Many of the prisoners come from the London area. With the advent of the M11 and improved main roads, their visitors often find that it takes far less longer than they imagined to reach Highpoint. Some, according to a number of prison officers, fill in the spare time by a spot of burglary at more isolated houses in the area.

The increase in burglary and car theft is undoubtedly one of the major aspects of change in Wickhambrook over the past quarter of a century. Even until ten years ago many people never bothered to lock their cars, even at night. House doors were often left unlocked during the day and burglary was still rare. Now we are a 'Neighbourhood Watch' area (one of Colin Bird's successes) and all busy fitting treble deadlocks on doors and windows.

However, not all of this can be laid at the door of Highpoint Prison. It is symptomatic of the nation's general moral decline, particularly in its declining respect for law and order, other people's rights and the old fashioned sense of duty.

How this came about, as with many other changes in a village's life pattern, together with an insight into the rich history of this part of the county, is now recorded in the extracts from the 'Wickhambrook Scene' from 1969 to 1994.

FROM THE 'WICKHAMBROOK SCENE'

February 1969

Extract from profile article on Alfred C. Hicks: 'The Scene's' most prolific contributor.

... By this time, World War II had arrived. He failed the Medical because of his toes and so, in view of his grocery experience, he offered his services to the NAAFI. He was based at Feltwell and Mildenhall throughout the War, but he cycled back to Wickhambrook every weekend!

When hostilities ceased he took up his present job as local agent for the Pearl Assurance Company. Until 10 years ago he used a bike to travel round the twenty villages in his area.

From when he gets up early in the morning until he goes to bed late at night Mr Hicks is working. However, his job with 'The Pearl' is only part of his work. As everybody knows, he joins in so many activities within the village that it would take all of this magazine to write about them. The diary which he has kept for 43 years must look very full indeed!

In spite of what the army thought, our man is certainly very fit. You need to be if you're a Football Referee. The game has changed since he finished playing for Wickhambrook when he was forty. Though there are too many squabbles over petty things and though players are more reluctant to accept discipline, he thinks the standard of play is much higher and there is still a good spirit in the game.

What has been the biggest change in village life over the last sixty years? People going outside the village to work, says Alf. Everyone living in Wickhambrook used to work here as well, but it's very different now. He does not want to see industry brought here to remedy the situation. People say Wickhambrook is ten miles from anywhere. 'How lovely', says Mr Hicks.

Report on Wickhambrook Football Personalities.
John S. Claydon – Captain and Right Back.
John, a 27 year old bachelor farmer, is a one-club player and the third generation of footballing Claydons to play for Wickhambrook. His father played in the 1930–40s and his grandfather in the 1920s.

Referred to by some as 'The Tank' John is a hard working, hard tackling right back who seems most effective when the going is heavy.

Steven C. Jolland – Forward.

Steve, a 26-year-old married man with two sons, became a regular player ten years ago. His first game for the team however, was when he was eleven years old. On that occasion Wickhambrook were beaten 19-0 by Brandon Town Street.

Steven is a fast forward with a powerful shot who prefers hard, dry pitches. He has scored 14 goals this season.

December 1994. Steve Jolland now has four sons. Mark, James and Nicholas all play for Wickhambrook Football Team, currently having one of its most successful seasons.

April 1969

Extract from profile article on Barry Pask. Then aged 21, his ancestors have lived in the village for three centuries.

There is a good Folk Club in Bury. The old songs passed on by word of mouth must be kept alive by clubs like this before it is too late. The same goes for the old Morris Dances which is another of his interests.

When he is not following this pastime or doing a bit of fishing he may be 'down the pub'. A country pub has a character of its own. People don't go there just to drink. It's a social centre with no class distinction. 'You can have a good old jaw even if you don't know the bloke you're talking to', says Barry.

Barry . . . thinks that local dialect is a good thing. 'Outsiders' are welcome to move into the village because they bring new ideas. Younger people are not so suspicious of outsiders as the older generation because the young folk tend to meet strangers to a greater extent in their work and play. At the same time they must remember they were not asked to come to Wickhambrook. Because of Barry's interest in the folk tradition he is also rather concerned that a large influx of outsiders would be the end of the local dialect.

June 1969

The names of the new Community Council Committee are published. Nineteen of the twenty-nine are local people by birth.

Mrs Jean Gardner (Chairman)
Mr John Long (Vice-Chairman)
Mr Peter Bayman (Hon. Secretary)
Mr Jack Mortlock (Hon. Treasurer)

Mr Percy Addison	Mr Frank Anderson	Mr Tommy Braker
Mr Harold Burton	Mr Bob Cook	Mr John Crysell
Mr Derrick Gee	Mrs Janet Gee	Mr John Green
Miss Carol Hart	Mrs Ivy Hicks	Mrs Esme Jolland
Mrs Elsie Jolly	Mrs Helen Long	Mr C. Reeve
Mr Len Rix	Mr Bill Saunders	Mrs Marina Savin
Mr Barry Shuter	Mr John Smith	Mr David Turner
Mr Bill Underwood		

A humorous anecdote in this issue in fact described several houses in the village at that time.

A young couple came to Wickhambrook to look at a house that was for sale. As they had been accustomed to living in the town they were surprised to find that the only tap was in the garden and there was no electricity.

Having seen the house, the young couple were finally shown the little building at the bottom of the garden.

'This is very primitive', said the young lady. 'There isn't even a lock on the door.'

'Oh, that's all right,' replied the old owner. 'I've been here for 30 years and no one has pinched the bucket yet!'

Also in the same June 1969 issue the then editor published an interview with Mrs Edith Claydon, a strong character who was still driving her own car until well into her eighties. Her two grandsons, who have three sons of their own between them, still farm in Wickhambrook today.

Mrs Claydon is really a newcomer to the village as she didn't arrive on the Wickhambrook scene until 1917!

However, for the last 52 years since her arrival there has been no family more widely known and more closely associated with the village than the Claydons.

The journey to Wickhambrook was not a very long one for Mrs Claydon. Her childhood was spent at Dunstall Green between Dalham and Ousden (three miles from Wickhambrook) where her father, Mr Bough, was first a gamekeeper and then took over her father-in-law's farm. The annual Flower Show at Ousden is one of her clearest memories. Most villages had their flower show in those days, with many attractions for the children including the steam-driven roundabouts and 'water-squirts' with which the boys drenched the girls!

Mrs Claydon's mother was also her tutor until, at the age of 12, she went to Mrs Petley's private school at Barrow. After leaving there when she was 15 life was filled with work at home, hockey and tennis. The First World War was soon here. It had its effect even in these parts. The Army called at the farms and commandeered all the best horses for military service. But the war didn't stop the tennis-playing and as a result Mrs Claydon met her husband-to-be, who was farming with his father at Witham's Farm, Wickhambrook. The young couple moved into the farmhouse in 1917 but it wasn't long before they had a chance to buy a place of their own. When Mr Tom Bowyer of Stradishall Manor died in 1920 a lot of land in Wickhambrook was put on the market. The Claydons were able to take this opportunity to buy Grove Farm, Attleton Green, when £25 per acre was a reasonable price for land.

This was a very different village in those days. The roads were very rough and narrow; the water was from a pump, a well or even a pond, and all hot water and hot food came from over the fire.

The summer of 1921 was so dry that Mr Claydon was cutting oats on 12th July. On that same day a fire started in a stack at Grove Farm which eventually destroyed all the buildings and gutted the house after burning for three days. At the start of the blaze Albert Haygreen sped off to Clare on his motor-bike to fetch the fire brigade but, by the time the horses had been caught and the tender drawn to Wickhambrook, little could be done.

On Christmas Day of that year a big crowd gathered in a meadow at Grove Farm. It was one of the first major football matches in the village, with Mr Claydon as Wickhambrook's first captain. The matches were played in the meadow until, with the help of Mr Fass of Giffords Hall and Dr Wilkin, the present Recreation Ground was made available.

Butlers Hall and Gains Hall became part of the Claydon's farming enterprise and then in 1943 came the addition of Boyden End where Mrs Claydon has lived ever since. By then this household was fortunate enough to have Calor Gas, water from a deep bore and even electricity from their own generating plant.

During the Second World War race-horses entered the family circle. With the help of trainers Harvey Leader and Bobby Jones the Claydons scored many successes at Kempton Park, Goodwood, Newmarket, York and other courses, particularly with their favourite horses 'Master of Boyden' and 'Boyden End'.

This war left its mark on Wickhambrook as did the first. As far as Mrs Claydon was concerned it meant a plane crash in a potato field and a bomb dropped on the house and buildings of their New England Farm. Mr Jack Ivans was living in the house at the time. When asked if he was hurt by the falling debris he replied, 'No, but it holly knocked my brussels sprouts about!'

Mrs Claydon lost her husband in 1955, but her seven children, most of whom live locally, have not let her become a lonely widow.

One of the major events of recent years was yet another fire which swept through the house at Boyden End in 1960. The tragedy was slightly lessened by an amusing incident. Mrs Claydon wanted to visit the smallest upstairs room at the height of the fire but the firemen advised her against it. Finally as the need for the visit became urgent, she was allowed to make the perilous journey . . . wearing a fireman's heavy coat and his helmet!

As you read this magazine Mrs Claydon's days at Boyden End are running out. She will soon be moving to a smaller house with a more manageable garden at Attleton Green.

We have said little yet of the major contribution Mrs Claydon has made to the social life of the village. No one has done as much

28

as Mrs Claydon to make life more interesting for the women of Wickhambrook. In the past she has been the guiding hand behind the Mothers' Union and the Girls' Friendly Society. She is now in her 7th year as President of the Women's Institute. When she attended the first meeting of the WI in 1926 she took her young baby with her. I don't suppose Mr Eric Claydon remembers much about the meeting!

Although there are now other attractions since the 'telly' arrived and cars have become common-place the WI still has an important role to play as an organisation which brings together all women regardless of class or religion. Mrs Claydon's main aim is to get all the members involved in running the many activities.

Here is a lady who could have led a very full and comfortable life without helping others. In fact, she has given up many, many hours of her time to see that other women in the village have had some pleasures and interest away from the kitchen sink.

August 1969

A report appears on future sewage schemes planned by Clare Rural District Council for Wickhambrook.

Subject to Ministry approval, it is hoped that mains drainage will be extended to a further two parts of the village in the near future. One extension will be from Clopton to Wickham Street and thence to a pumping station behind the Plumber's Arms . . . The other extension will start beyond the new bungalows at Attleton Green. From the Green it will follow the line of the brook to Woollard's Corner and there link up with the present system.

When I moved in at Attleton Green in 1973 this second mains drainage had just been completed. However, the previous owner had forgotten to see that our house was connected to it. We discovered this omission, preceded by several weeks of peculiar odours during August of that year, when what we thought was a defunct septic tank began to well up in the middle of the lawn.

In the same issue there is a profile on Brenda and Roger Fairhall, who had then lived in the village some two years after keeping a pub in Surrey for 15 years. Roger died in 1978. Brenda is currently Vice-Chairman of the Parish Council. They also have something to say on septic tanks in that 1969 report.

. . . Wickhambrook has two disadvantages over some of the places where the Fairhalls have lived. First, having no sewer is a nuisance if your septic tank is not efficient. Secondly, there are few footpaths by the roads and limited or discontinued rights of way across the fields. Though Roger has noticed that Wickhambrook still has its 'gentry' on the one hand and the 'working people' on the other, relations between the two parties are good, with many people of both groups playing an active part together in the community.

After 15 years as a publican, Roger shows considerable interest in local hostelries and their habitues. What does he think of the ones here? First, people go more for the company and less for the drink. 'I've never seen anyone really "sloshed" here,' says Roger. Secondly, there is no division into Saloon and Public trade. Everyone mingles together in the same room.

What about Wickhambrook tomorrow? How will it differ from Wickhambrook today? They think there will be many more people like themselves coming here from other parts of the country.

October 1969
Peter Rodwell, who then lived in Brook Cottage, opposite the Cloak Inn, gave extracts from the day books and diaries of a certain Dr Stutter who lived in Brook Cottage in the 19th Century.

'RECOLLECTIONS OF DR STUTTER'
To the long-established Wickhambrookian, Brook Cottage is 'Dr Stutter's house'. Day books found in the roof show that certainly one Dr Stutter was practising during the period 1842–1867.

One of the most interesting of the records found is an unsigned and undated petition in fine copperplate handwriting. It reads as follows:-

> *To the Honourable the Board for Administration the Poor Law of Great Britain, Somerset House*
> The humble petition of the undersigned Guardians and other Ratepayers of the several parishes of Stansfield, Denardiston, Stradishall, Wickhambrook and Cowlinge, forming a part of the Risbridge Union occupying the number of acres attached to their names herewith.
> That your petitioners together with several members of their families have been professionally attended by Mr William Gaskoin Stutter who has acted as Medical Attendant to the above Parishes since 1842.
> That your petitioners have always felt satisfied no less with the professional skill than the personal attention of the aforesaid Gentleman who has been equally fortunate in cases demanding surgical operations as in those requiring medical treatment.
> That your petitioners have lately heard with equal surprise and regret that another Gentleman, viz Mr Benjamin Baker of Thurlow has been elected in the place of Mr Stutter, their regret being aggravated by the consciousness that such latter election was carried out by a majority of the

Haverhill Board of Guardians, utterly unconnected with the above mentioned parishes; whilst *all* the Guardians appointed on behalf of the said Parishes voted unanimously for the said Mr Stutter.

That your petitioners most humbly submit to your Honourable Board whether such majority of Guardians had not some *personal motive* for such election which ought to be fully made known for the satisfaction of your petitioners.

That your petitioners having the means of payment for Medical attendance, are perfectly indifferent to the latter appointment with regard *merely to themselves* but they feel in duty bound to respect the conscientious objections and honest remonstrances of a *very extensive* number of the residents in the afore-mentioned parishes.

District of Labouring Poor who make no secret in declaring their utter want of confidence and personal dislike in respect of their new Medical attendant, whilst on the contrary they express their deepest anxiety in the re-election of the aforesaid Mr Stutter.

That your petitioners most humbly entreat your Honourable Board not to confirm the latter election of Medical Officer by the Haverhill Board but to re-elect the aforesaid Mr Stutter to his former position.

And your petitioners as in duty bound will ever pray.'

And their follows spaces for signatures.

Is this a copy of a petition which was actually presented? Or did Dr Stutter suppress a document drawn up by anxious friends on the grounds that he wanted nothing further to do with the affair? Or did he concoct it himself, and was he unable to persuade anyone to sign it?

Haverhill Council have no record of the matter. In course of time I shall see if Somerset House have any record of the affair. It might well have become an important issue in the local politics of the time.

Further extracts from Dr Stutter's diaries appeared in November 1984.

In the same issue of 'The Scene' the Chairman reported on the progress in the major developments for the expansion of the village's 'Memorial Hall'.

... May we also remember that it will always be 'The Memorial Hall', that it means more to us than bricks and mortar, and will serve Wickhambrook for many years in the way the original benefactors intended ... We still have a long way to go financially before we complete our plans for the hall improvements and so we ask you all again for your continued support in all our activities and efforts for success.

February 1970

The vicar of All Saints Church, the Reverend John Hodgson,
announced his retirement after eight years. Born in Co.
Durham in 1903 he went to New Zealand in 1920 and was
ordained priest there in 1930.

HEARE MAI

On the night we arrived from our parish in Derbyshire, I traced the key of the (Wickhambrook) Vicarage in a builder's hut, after stumbling into a large hole and was thus introduced to the clinging quality of Wickhambrook clay. Our furniture had preceded us, but the plug of the electric kettle was different so rather than face the night tea-less, we set off to find Denston Rectory. The Rector and his family were out, so some hour or more later we arrived back at the Vicarage still cold and without 'a cuppa'. So we set off again to find lodgings, finishing after eleven o'clock at the 'Angel' in Bury. I think I find my way now, but am still doubtful about directing a stranger for fear he lands in Farley Green when he wants to go to Genesis Green.

Sometimes I have wished there was more of a village centre but most times I am glad that the 'Wickhambrook Scene' is so diverse, because of the many viewing points of beauty and serenity during all seasons of the year. Naturally after many years of exile since our return ten years ago, my wife and I have visited most parts of Britain but as we pass the Plumbers Arms and approach the cluster of homes around the Church, I wonder why we bother to go sight-seeing when the essence of the 'home' country is daily within sight of the Vicarage windows.

Rudyard Kipling in a poem written nearly seventy years ago begins:-

> God gave all men all earth to love
> But since our hearts are small
> Ordained for each, one spot should prove
> Beloved over all'.

He was thinking of Sussex; I almost think the same of Wickhambrook and am quite certain anyone born and bred here ought to do.

There was a church on the present site of All Saints before 1066, so I can claim spiritual ancestry through my predecessors way back to our Saxon forbearers. So, despite my tea-less beginning, to accept newcomers very early on in my ministry I felt at one with you, and now feel one of you and know that my memory of you will be as tenacious as Wickhambrook clay itself.

I began with the Maori cry of welcome and goodwill, so finish with their goodbye of all the best for you and yours.

Kia.............Ora

When the Rev. Hodgson retired he was succeeded by the Rev.
Bill Davis, who after 24 years is due to retire in early 1995. A

dedicated priest, Bill Davis expects those who wish to marry, or have their offspring baptised, within his church to at least have some understanding of the Christian beliefs behind the appropriate service. If they show that they have no wish to understand those beliefs, then he lets it be known that they can go elsewhere. This has given him his critics as well as his supporters. The former will point out that he was eager enough to give constant attendance upon the Moslem, Hindu and Sikh Ugandan Asians based at the former RAF Stradishall in 1972 with little hope of any conversions to Christianity. Perhaps Bill Davis recognised that at least the Asians had a belief.

As well as the Rev. Hodgson, Christopher Antony was also expressing his feelings on the antiquity of Wickhambrook in that February 1970 issue of 'The Scene'.

... Almost certainly the scattered nature of our village betrays its history. And unless I am much mistaken, it is a history of great antiquity, a history humble no doubt, but proud. For Wickhambrook belongs to High Suffolk, the clay uplands of the county once covered by oak forest. Look around the village! You will still see the remnants of the forest in the few great oaks that remain. If our Suffolk oaks had been protected by the king, which they were not, we might have had Robin Hood in Wickhambrook. Instead the trees were felled – apart from one giant in my garden which must have been a sizeable fellow when the abbey at Bury was still one of the greatest shrines in Christendom. Ships and homes and churches grew from the fallen oaks, and trees in a sense live on in many a house in Wickhambrook to this day.

Wheat replaced the oak and I doubt if there is better corn land in all England than the rich clay of Suffolk.

I fancy it was the Saxons, a mere thousand years ago or so, who really decided the shape and character of Wickhambrook. They began to clear the forest and build fortified farmhouses that may well have been the ancestors of 'halls' like Giffords and Badmondisfield and several hundred more in High Suffolk. As time passed, the village grew up, not in a close cluster for purposes of water supply, communications, shelter or defence, but around a series of large and scattered farms. At least that's my theory!

April 1970

Jack Mortlock writes on the area covered by Wickhambrook, with his first paragraph spelt as Suffolk dialect is pronounced.

Wickham is a grut owd village bur – I heered its the biggest in Suffolk – over seven miles acraws. Dam it bur – there are seven or ight 'Greens'. You look – that's a tidy ould step from Wickham Strit up there to the other side er Genesis Green dam nie inter Lidgate. I

33

walked that one arter-nun. Left Wickham Strit bout harf arter tew dam it – it were arter faur afare I git there.

The greatest distance to be apart and still be in Wickhambrook is 4 miles 295 yards between Lady's Green and the boundary of a field at Farley Green on the left of the road just beyond Moat Farm. By road it is 5½ miles. From Lady's Green to the boundary down at Wickham House is just 200 yards shorter.

Round the boundary of the village it is approximately 17 miles. The highest point in the village is between Black Horse Farm and the Water Tower at Ashfield Green at 404 feet.

June 1970

Great relief is expressed in the editorial that the plans for the Memorial Hall have been approved.
It is good to have the long awaited letter of approval from London. I think many of us were beginning to lose heart at the delay over the plans for the Memorial Hall and I am sure you will agree with me that now we have the go ahead even greater efforts are required by all of us to get the project started and even more important to see it finished.

I believe the project has great possibilities primarily for the Community, but also for much wider use. Let us therefore make it our business as subscribers to see that every possible angle of the project has been thoroughly assessed and that we can be assured our money is being spent wisely, not just for us but for future generations.

Alf Hicks submits his report from the Horticultural Society, with a major 'plug' for the Flower Show and Carnival on July 11th.
One of the judges choosing our Carnival Queen and attendants will be Wing Commander G. K. Bushell from RAF Stradishall. In the Show there are 100 classes of fruit, vegetables and flowers you can enter.

In the past the Show has been held in various places, including Stradishall and Denston Hall. In its Golden Jubilee year, 50 years ago nearly, it was at Giffords Hall, then the home of the late A. H. Fass, a keen Vice President of the Society. For many years now the venue has been the Recreation Ground at Wickhambrook.

In our early years some of us remember with affection the meadow behind the vicarage and Church where the Show was held for a number of years. 'Stinger' Wright's Fair struggling through the soft ground and mud to get on the spot and vowing 'never to come again'. One can still hear the strains of 'I'm forever blowing bubbles', 'Valencia' and other tunes as the steam horses went round and round to the sound of an occasional whistle.

Here besides the prize vegetables etc., were thrilling athletic events including pole jump and the start of stirring contests of six-a-side football, with Ernie Nelson, Jack Alexander, Fred Littlechild, Eric

McKenzie, Lewis Hurrell, Tom Claydon and others doing heroics for Wickhambrook.

A report is published from Jack Mortlock on 'The Cloak' Knock-Out Dominoes Cup.

This competition is well under way – there are 32 entrants for this Knock-Out and the three previous holders of the cup were all knocked out in the early rounds. They were Paul Harrod, Norton Hicks and Charlie Pettitt. Three players are already through to the semi-final: Peter Mortlock (*Jack's youngest son*), a thoughtful young player; Les Hurrell, a crafty player from Nunnery Green and Roger Fairhall an experienced player who knows every trick in the book.

August 1970

A further article is published on Wickhambrook's non-conformist traditions, where Congregationalists – now United Reform Church – first met in a barn at the beginning of the 18th Century.

FROM BARN TO CHAPEL

The Rev. Thomas Priest came to the Barn in 1726 and although he kept no minutes he commenced a Book of Baptisms and it states:- 'Thomas Priest preached his first Sermon in the Old Meeting House at Badmondisfield Hall 6th August 1726.'

Before he was ordained 8 children were baptized by other Ministers, the first being – 13th August 1726. 'Elizabeth, dau. of Daniel Park and Elizabeth his wife (who died in childbirth) by Rev. Mr Green of Haverhill. The 7th Baptism was actually by the Rev. Mr Grant, Vicar of Wickhambrook, which was remarkable at that time.

Then we are told:- 'Thos. Priest was publicly ordained to the Ministry ... 1728 in the Meeting House at Badmondisfield (commonly called Bansfield) by the Revs Messrs Thomas Steward of St Edmundsbury (afterwards D.D.) ...' and several other Ministers.

Thomas Steward was the Presbyterian Minister at Bury. Mr Priest carried out several Baptisms 'in the Meeting House' in 1728, but from the beginning of 1729 most of the baptisms were 'privately' (that is, in private houses) and they were at Denston, Cowlinge, Lidgate, Ousden, Rede, Chevington, Hargrave and Hundon up to 1734 in addition to those at Wickhambrook.

79 Baptisms were recorded in that period and in addition to the name Pask we have as parents – Past, Simpson, Sparrow, Hart, Pond, Rawling and Henry and Mary Edgeley, etc.

Mr Priest married in 1730 Elizabeth Cradock, daughter of Walter Cradock and granddaughter of Samual Cradock and went to live at Gesyns which he had bought from Mr Walter Cradock.

The work in the Barn had prospered and Mr Priest had gone out into all the villages.

In 1734 he set on foot a Collection for the erection of a Chapel and this was built to accommodate 300 at a cost of £405.5.11. The subscription fell short by £132.15.5 and Mr Priest must have paid the remainder.

The Licence for the chapel was as follows:- Wickhambrook 2nd October 1734. 'It was certified by John Hinton of Hargrave that a new building situate in Wickhambrook abutting South West on the house of Joseph Cook, and North East on the house of John Pearson is set apart for the religious worship of Protestant Dissenters'.

Thus from the house at Gesyns, then from the Barn at Badmondisfield Hall this congregation of Dissenting Worshippers had arrived at their own Chapel where they still worship today.

In the August 1970 issue there was also an advertisement for the Harvest Horkey, to be held in the Memorial Hall on October 23rd. It was to be 'a real Old Fashioned Horkey with Sing-Song, Sketches and Humour'. Those with talent were asked to contact Jack Mortlock at the Cloak.

All major farmers in the area held their own Harvest Horkeys for their workers and their families up until the mid-Thirties. The tradition was continued in the Memorial Hall but with the accelerating decline in the number of people working on the land, plus the competition of other forms of entertainment and the fact that the background of half the population today of the village is now 'town' rather than 'country', the old Harvest Horkey is now dead.

We were fortunate enough to attend what were probably the last two that had some semblance of their original meaning in 1973 and 74. Whole families were there, with entertainment in song, dance, music and 'rustic recitations' being provided by granddaughters and grandfathers – and many a barrel of Greene King's ale being emptied.

December 1970

A letter from Miss Dulcie Smith paints the background to the plans for the Village Memorial Hall.

No date could be more appropriate than 1970 for a few words here about Wickhambrook's Village Hall, for it marks the Silver Jubilee – not of the hall itself, but of the first idea of it. Twenty-five years ago I wrote in my diary at Giffords Hall that 'a Mr Underwood' had come to see Miss Stagg and me about a proposal from 'a Mr Leonard Harbutt' that the village War Memorial should take the form of a village hall. Willie Underwood, Alfred Hicks and others will no doubt remember a public meeting on Jan. 23rd 1945 at which the idea was taken up, and at another meeting some three weeks later when the recreation ground trustees decided to offer a site on the ground for the hall. Our architect was not far to seek, for Hope Bagenal's daughter was with me on Giffords Farm, and said 'I think Daddy would like to design your hall if it's to be a War Memorial'. He did, and waived his fee for that reason, having lost a son in the war. In the following May the proposed site was approved by Hope Bagenal, and the Village Hall idea was off to a flying start.

That flight was not without its hazards during the years which followed, but on May 18th 1950, Hope Bagenal was on the recreation ground discussing details with the builders (Harvey Frost) and two months later the hall was ready to be christened as a village meeting place by the first meeting of the newly constituted VH Working Committee. It might have been well and truly christened in the orthodox way, for as yet it had no roof, but luckily the weather was fine. And before long Mrs Dawson's gift of the beautiful Suffolk-black tiles disposed of that hazard.

The rest of the story is a tale of money raising schemes, already begun by the first carnival in 1945, and continued throughout the years.

A profile on another village personality was published in this issue, following an interview by Jack Mortlock.

ROBERT THOROGOOD was born 78 years ago at Attleton Green, on 25th August 1892.

'Old Bob' still leads a very active life and gets a great deal of pleasure from his garden, riding his 'owd boyke' and watching the village football team. He left Attleton Green as a baby to live in a cottage at Blue Doors Farm, Stradishall, returned to Wickhambrook at the age of nine to live at Coltsfoot Green, and from there had his first regular job at the age of 14 on Australia Farm at ninepence a day! 'Cleaning mangols, swids and lookin' arter an old pig or tew'. He then took a better paid job at Ashfield Hall at 1/-, for a 10 hour day, and this he continued to do until he joined the Suffolk Regiment at the beginning of the First World War.

In those days most of the men of the village were known by a nickname and Bob's family will be remembered by some of our older readers. His father was 'Whistler', his mother Liza, oldest brother Harry was 'Nobs', brother Ben was 'Ben Zoo' and Humphrey was 'Towser'.

The summer of 1914 was a fine one and the harvest was completed in record time – mowing was done by hand and saile machine, the sheaves were tied by hand. Harvest except the 'rakings' was in by the end of August. Bob, very keen to get into the Army, didn't wait to collect his harvest bonus, gave instructions for it to be paid to his mother and set out to walk to Bury, accompanied by his brother Ben, and a friend Harry Stiff (later killed in action). They had several drinks on the road and by the time they had reached the 'Spread Eagle' pub at Bury were so drunk they decided to retrace their steps back to the 'bench oak' tree at Horringer and spent the night in a field. Here Ben, who had had a bit of service in the Militia before the war, gave the other two the slip and returned to Wickhambrook. Bob and his companion proceeded back to the barracks at Bury and joined up.

Bob served through the war in France, Egypt and Greece and has three medals to his credit. He came on leave once during those years and had to walk from Newmarket station in full kit including rifle. During this leave he tells me that he met a rather nice girl at the bottom of Fullers Hill. He took her to Bury, bought her a ring and told her to wait for him until the war was over. Her name was Elsie Smith who later became his wife and the mother of his two sons Algy and Maurice and two daughters Olga and Freda.

After the war Bob and his new wife settled down at Ashfield Green and lived comfortably in a disused railway carriage: the dining room was first class, the bedroom a non-smoker.

Bob, now a widower, lives at Coltsfoot Green and looks after himself. He enjoys his pipe and an occasional Guinness. Thirty years ago Bob was fitted with false teeth – he used them once. Since then he has kept them in a jam-jar. He seems to manage very well without a tooth in his head. Good Luck to you Bob 'old timer', may we see you around the village for a very long time to come.

Concluding the December issue was a report on the Harvest Horkey held in October. It gave local comments, with interpretations for non-Suffolk speakers.

LOCAL	*INTERPRETATION*
'Tha were bloody gud'	'Excellent'
'Ie larft til Ie croyd'	'Hilarious'
'Thum therr birrds flappin and a squawkin'	'Entertaining'
'Bes ten bob Ieever did spen'	'Worth it'
'Tha therr Len Rix were holly gud'	'Personal Best'
'Fud, Ie aint sin so much fud since yearts'	'Impressive'
'Tha were wor evry penny on i'	'Inexpensive'
'Hey ya ga a ly ba'	'Realistic'

One organiser at the Horkey went out the front door of the Memorial Hall. On seeing two shapes on the grass he went to investigate. A punch-up or snoggers? Neither. On approaching one ran off, the other shape stayed very still. It was a keg of beer on the way to the other shape's car boot.

April 1971
The editor, writing in his column, recognises that change in a village is inevitable.
. . . We know and like our village as it really is. Change is inevitable but we must not have the village or our lives spoilt by it without our

notice. The onus is on us to keep up and be aware of the facts. It's our village Wickhambrookians. Let's keep it that way.

It was with deep regret that we learnt in February of the death of Miss Dulcie Lawrence Smith...

We are sure all our committee and readers extend a very warm welcome to (*the new vicar*) Mr and Mrs W. H. Davis and family.

August 1971

The first airing of views on the likelihood of a prison in the area came in the editorial.

... The EEC and the possible prison coming to the ex-RAF Station are two major talking points. Does anyone know the full implications of either? Provided both are beneficial to the community they could be faced with a little more acceptance.

With regard to Stradishall Aerodrome, there is to be an early meeting of Local Authorities in consultation with the interested Government departments. We will do our best to listen to local opinion and assist in any positive approach as the necessity and occasion arises. Do we for instance favour the probability that the many acres should return to farm land? Are the buildings on both side of the road suitable for an open prison?

A stop press item announced that the contract for the Village Memorial Hall extensions had been formally signed and the work should be completed in nine months time.

October 1971

The editor announces with enthusiasm that following the signing of the contract work has begun on the Memorial Hall extensions. He also bemoans the fact that at that time there were no regulations controlling straw burning at harvest time.

Things are at long last happening. Yes, work has started on the Memorial Hall project. This you will be pleased to hear. Situated as it is near the road we can all watch eagerly the progress over the months. Now the cry will be 'When will it be finished!?' Within 9 months according to the contract.

One which is not such a pleasant sight is the farmers' annual burn-up of hedges and trees. Is it not possible with just a little extra time and care to control this annual devastation? As custodians of the countryside it is the farmers' duty to keep the hedgerows looking beautiful. Many of us value the birds and small animals that are destroyed at this time.

In the report from the secretary of the Horticultural Society concern is expressed over a new trend: people coming in to the Summer Show without paying.

... We are hoping to make a small profit on the Summer Show but expenses were considerably higher this year. There were a few 'leakages' from spectators who got in without paying. However, we feel confident we can tighten up next year!

At our last meeting members expressed appreciation for all the hard work put in by the Women's Institute in running the teas and the Community Council for selling hot dogs and organising a bar.

With Remembrance Sunday approaching two villagers recalled their experiences of Armistice Day 1918 and VE Day 1945.

ARMISTICE 1918 by Charlie Pettitt

Armistice Day! I was in Belgium as a driver with Royal Field Artillery. Finished firing our guns at 11 a.m. on 11th November 1918 right up against the infantry, who were in front of us, and shells were dropping all around the battery until 11 o'clock from the German guns. Horses and mules arrived; I was on the horses. We moved straight on into Metternich in Germany, about 4 days journey.

We picketed the horses each night, sleeping and stopping where we could but had the best time afterwards, good food and properly billeted in Germany and I was there for three years afterwards.

I joined up in 1918 and went into the Saar in France in the snow. Landed at Le Havre to find Chambery and Monchy all smashed to smithereens, nothing left standing. I was in the firing line for six or seven months and I shall never forget the poor wretches lying in the mud: bodies everywhere. I remember a long thin line of us, French and British, stretched right across the country for miles and miles and the mules played up at the noise as we crossed the makeshift pontoon bridges, and many of them went into the canals too, under fire all the time.

One afternoon there were 10 or 12 of us playing cards on the grass and we heard a shell coming over which was one of our own – a dud. It was in the ground before we could even duck.

I only had one home leave at Lady's Green (Wickhambrook) until 1920.

Work was a bit short when I was demobbed and the first job I had was at Rowland Marsh's of Hungriff, cutting and tying flax, which was hung and dried in the barn over there.

VE DAY 1945 by Percy Nunn

My memories of May 8th 1945 have become somewhat hazy but I do have some recollection of that day. I was in Bremen, with the British Liberation Army, that North German city having just fallen to the Allied Forces. We had been detailed that morning to pick up a detachment of American troops and transport them to some obscure part of the front. Picking our way through the scenes of utter devastation we located them at about 10 a.m.

'Relax, buddies, it's all over! Cease Fire was 8 a.m.,' they shouted, and we endured much back-slapping, hand-shaking, and of course, the usual lavish American hospitality. We eventually completed our devious journey, but seeing the war-ravaged countryside it gradually began to sink in just how tragically unnecessary it had all been. I thought of my wife and small daughter in Scotland. Somehow they felt even more precious to me now.

Arriving back at our unit we were greeted with smiling faces. 'Yes, the war is over in Europe, and what do you think! We've found an air-raid shelter stacked to the roof with Rhine wine! Boy, oh Boy, we're having the party of all parties tonight!' WE DID.

December 1971
Excitement in the village as people can now begin to see the shape of the new Memorial Hall extensions as they rise from the footings.

We are now able to see the shape and size of the various rooms around the Memorial Hall. It is now possible to walk around and stand in them and try and work out what is what.

On A. Bailey and Sons' side (South), there is the club room, with a modernised and enlarged kitchen and adjoining servery. There is a sliding partition access into the main hall. The small room to the rear is the heating/boiler room.

On the Women's Institute side (North), there is the committee room. To the rear there are two storage rooms – one with access to the main hall only and the other with access onto the recreation ground.

On the front there is the foyer entrance, with an open cloakroom and on the other side the ladies and gentlemen's toilet accommodation.

Let us hope for a mild winter so that there is no hold up for bad weather. We shall plan for a gala opening in April. Ideas for this will be welcomed by the Hall Committee.

Perhaps with one eye on the newcomers to the village, Len Rix writes an article on farming, which he entitles 'Farming – Or How I Prefer To Live With The Bean'

What is a farm? To most people, especially townsfolk, it is a quaint old house with a pond nearby and ducks swimming on it. There is a stockyard with hens scratching in the straw and an old pig looking over his sty. Then there is the meadow with half a dozen cows of various colours grazing the grass.

To some it even includes the old horse looking over his stable door, but most people realise that tractors are the thing nowadays.

We in the country know differently and that farmers specialize in one or two enterprises only. Dairy farms with 100 to 200 cows are commonplace and pig farms with 1,000 pigs or more are the thing. Sheep are mainly used on large arable farms in this part of the country to utilise break crops and to help soil fertility. And a one acre poultry farm could hold 20,000 laying hens, so it's obvious times have changed.

But what of the future? All these animals produce food for us to eat but of course they must live themselves. Therefore a large part of the food they eat goes to maintaining them in good condition which is wasteful of resources.

So scientists have found ways of processing vegetable matter into acceptable human food, even to simulating taste and texture of traditional food like meat and milk. Needless to say, this food can be produced much more cheaply than that produced by livestock enterprises, efficient though they may be.

Now it's time for the crystal ball and a peep into the future. Does it show vast acreages of beans or oil seed rape or green vegetables grown for the giant processing factories, with extensive use of artificial fertilizer? Does it show even more hedgerows bulldozed out to create even bigger fields, with absent fences to keep in the absent cow and sheep? Or will it be a compromise, as we have already found in the butter vs marge concept, with meat still being eaten say once a week and real cream and dairy produces being used but rather as a luxury.

Myself, I hope that my grandchildren stand as good a chance of getting muck on their boots as I have, but who knows.

February 1972

The nineteen forties GI Brides of East Anglia are legendary. With many US Air Bases being retained throughout the cold war period there has been a substantial second and third generation of GI Brides, again many of them coming from the West Suffolk area.

The following letter appeared in the 'Junior Scene' – namely, contributions from Wickhambrook school.

MY TRIP TO ENGLAND

Well, it started in Oklahoma when we got orders to go to Washington State. It was car all the way but we didn't worry as the Forces paid for the gas.

We got there in five days and were there for seven months. It was fun but we had to go on again, this time by plane. I was scared at first, but in three hours we were in Kansas City where it was 8 degrees below zero. We took off for Philadelphia and then went by car to McGuire Air Force Base. Oh, did it ever feel so good to be in a car again!

At midnight we were back on the plane; this time a different plane, even bigger and better. In the morning I was the first awake except for the crew. I was sitting by the window and saw some islands. Soon we were landing at Mildenhall Air Base. Our grandparents were there to meet us.

I couldn't believe I was home again!

Andy Yates.

Elsewhere in this issue another insight is given to village life in the early years of this century in an article by Gwen Dennis.

My father, Rev. A. McKechnie, was vicar of Wickhambrook for nearly 50 years and through him I have many memories of a bygone way of life. We were '10 miles from anywhere' and with practically no transport, not even to Bury, we lived our own lives in the Community.

. . . One bridegroom had failed to bring a ring to the Church and as nothing else could be found, my father married them with the Church key slipped on the bride's finger. If you know the size and weight of this key, you would hope that the bride didn't wear her 'ring' too long!

In the vestry after the ceremony the groom was confiding to the vicar that he had no idea why he had got married: 'Tain't for love and tain't for beauty,' he said. One can only hope that the bride did not hear these heart-searchings.

With the White House, then the White Horse Inn, opposite the Old Vicarage, we were very much aware of what was happening there.

One day the bar door was thrust open and there was a lot of shouting, followed by a woman crying loudly at the top of her voice. She came straight to the Vicarage, where my father met her in the garden and she then threw herself into his arms and sobbed: 'Why should I be degraded?' She had been turned out for being hopelessly drunk and had come across for comfort from one who, she said: 'I always look on as a kind of father.'

I don't think he was very proud of his 'kind of daughter', but he was very touched that she came straight to him.

Another time, one summer's evening about 1920, a professional agitator came to talk and the men came out, pints in hand, and listened quietly. After a long harangue the speaker asked if they had any questions for him. Dead silence. Then one man said: 'Yes Guvner. Where do flies go in the wintertime? Do they go to Gay Paree?' (quoting a current song hit). Loud laughter and then back to the bar after such thirsty work.

One winter's night there was great merriment outside the pub's club room. One member was rather the worse for wear, so his friends went outside for a few minutes, then knocked on the door and said: 'Your carriage, sir' and escorted him to a waiting wheelbarrow and shoved him home.

The Sunday School Treat, held in the Glebe meadow, was one of the Summer's events. Days before we all said it *must* be fine on the

43

day, and it usually was. Swings, sports, tea at long trestle tables, prizes and a scramble for sweets.

Talking of the tea reminds me of the time my father drove in a pony trap to Bury to get things for the treat and especially for pounds of rich fruit slab cake. When he returned my mother unpacked the things and asked where the cake was. Cake? He had forgotten to get any! Doubtless Woollards (then the village shop) helped out as best as they could.

TUMBRILS AT WOOLLARDS CORNER

Just two pages on in this first issue of 1972 there was a letter from Mr Jack Woollard announcing the closing of the family shop.
A new shop would be opened by Mr Jim Mayes and his family from Surrey. In 1994 the 'new shop' is still going strong and is now managed by Jim's daughter, Barbara.

My grandfather, T. R. Woollard, started this business at Cutbush, Wickhambrook in about 1862 or 63 according to the oldest insurance policies I can find. In 1866 he moved to Commerce House where the business has carried on ever since. In the circular he sent round informing people of this 'Removal of Business', he gave his 'sincere thanks for the liberal support he had received from his numerous friends and hoped that the supply of good articles at reasonable prices will ensure a continuance of their patronage and the constant favour of the public generally.'

In 1914 my grandfather died and my father, Percy Woollard, who had been in the business since leaving school, took over control. The experience of rationing and dealing with food shortages which he gained during the 1914–18 war proved invaluable during the difficult years of the Second World War.

When I was a boy, deliveries used to be by horse-drawn van and pony cart. Paraffin was delivered in barrels on a dray drawn by horses.

All goods that came by rail were collected from Clare Station (to be closed by Dr Beeching) by the horses and tumbrils from the farm. The two men doing this used to groom and feed the horses, milk the cows and feed the pigs, before setting off to Clare in the morning, arriving back in the afternoon in time to attend to the animals again. This used to happen once or twice a week.

In 1922 we graduated to a 1913 model T Ford van which we ran for about ten years – made of very different stuff from the cars of today!

In 1924 when I started work in the business, we used to be open from 8 a.m. to 7 p.m. on Monday, Tuesday and Wednesday, half-day on Thursday, then 8 a.m. to 8 p.m. on Friday and 8 a.m. to 9 p.m. on Saturday.

In those days, like most village general stores, we used to sell a large amount of men's and lady's clothing, hats, suits, etc. This trade gradually declined and after the Second World War became only a small part of the business.

Now I am retiring at the end of this month and would like to take this opportunity of thanking all our customers for their loyal support. Quite a number of these were already dealing with us when I started work in 1924 and are real old friends.

Many thanks also to a very loyal staff, three of whom, Bert and Joan Pask and George Long, have been here for over 25 years!

Mr Mayes of Thorns Corner is going to continue in giving the same service to Wickhambrook and district and I wish him every success in the future.

Jack Woollard.

The bottom of Shop Hill, where the Woollard family lived for over a hundred years, is still known as 'Woollards Corner'.

April 1972

The Editor writes:

I make no apology for mentioning the Memorial Hall project. As the work continues, with men of various trades coming and going, there is an air of turning the last bend into the straight with three furlongs to go.

With carpet, curtains, tiles and paint colours all chosen, the finishing touches are put into operation with nearly all the construction work completed.

The official opening of the replanned, redecorated and refurnished hall takes place at 6 p.m. on Saturday 27th May. Our Member of Parliament, Mr Eldon Griffiths, has very kindly agreed to be present and undertake the official opening ceremony.

You will be kept informed of the decisions we make for further celebrations during the same evening. Watch for our usual notices and keep your ears to the underground telegraph.

Alf Hicks, writing as Hon. Secretary of the Horticultural Society, makes a plea for support for the coming Carnival and Flower Show day in July.

Spring has been in the air these last few days and gardeners have been busy preparing for the Show to be held on the recreation ground on Saturday 8th July,.

Opportunity knocks. Many people, of course, only 'turn over the garden' in their mind. Think not of football or of cricket now the trees have buds. For the time has come for putting in those spuds.

Please be thinking about the Carnival and ideas for entries, decorated vehicles and fancy dress. We have booked bands and hope to see a long procession. There were 14 entries last year, make it 20 or over this year!

We could do with more helpers on the day of the show. We have one of the best village shows in Suffolk. With the full support of all the worthy citizens of Wickhambrook and District it could become sensational!

September 1972

Five pages of this issue are devoted to the official opening of the Memorial Hall, or Memorial Social Centre as it should be known officially. Peter Bayman, the Community Council Chairman, gave a detailed account of the events leading to its completion. He then handed over the key to 'Madam Chairman', Mrs Gardner, who would in today's non-sexist society be addressed as 'The Chairperson' or 'The Chair' – neither of which to me show the respect of 'Madam Chairman'.

Mrs Gardner revealed that the Memorial Hall represented an investment by the village of 'at least £40,000, which is an amazing achievement for a village the size of Wickhambrook.'

In the Secretary's report in this issue on the August Meeting of the Community Council Committee it stated that 'Owing to the Harvest many committee members were absent.'

An indication of the occupational changes among committee members is that at the August 1993 Committee Meeting only one member was absent due to Harvest work: Peter Bayman.

November 1972

A list of Suffolk dialect names for birds and animals was published. It stated that 'many of these names are no longer in common usage.' Today, to my knowledge not one is. I felt that the following examples were particularly descriptive.

Bullfinch – blood elp	Long-tailed tit – pudden-e-poke
Curlew – thick knees	Owl – jilly hooter
Duck – diddles	Rabbit - batsy
French partridge – red ligs	Hare - owd sally
Hedge sparrow – hedge betty	Frog - hopnett

July 1973

With the major extensions to the Memorial Hall now fully completed, there now appeared in the 'Scene' the first reference to the plans to more than double the size of the recreation ground. Greeted with almost unanimous enthusiasm at the time, twenty years later, with the greatly expanded recreation facilities available, it was to cause division in the village.

Some feared that the large grants given for its development were a trojan horse from St Edmundsbury Council for major development of the village itself.

The report was on the June meeting of the Community Council.

At an extraordinary meeting, Mr John Long, Community Council Chairman, reported on the progress in the purchase of land at the bottom of the existing Recreation Ground. A letter from the Parish Council was read setting out the Council's willingness to buy the land from the Community Council for the village, provided a grant from the Department of the Environment was available, at the price paid by them. It was necessary for us to pay a deposit on the land by 7th June whilst the Parish Council sorted out the legal and financial position.

Mr Reed proposed and Mr Davis seconded that we buy the land, 6.4 acres at the price offered at £400 per acre, for £2,600, and carry the purchase through whether or not the Parish Council obtain the grant. Passed unanimously.

At the end of the report on the Community Council it stated:
The following were to be approached to see if they would join the Community Council Committee: Mr and Mrs Adams, Mrs Jones, Mr John Bean.

October 1973

CHANGES IN POLICE RURAL PATROL COVER

Up to now Wickhambrook, like most Suffolk villages of any size, had its own resident Police Constable. In our case it was David Turner, later to become Sergeant, who was also a prominent member of the Community Council, the Hall Committee and the Methodist Chapel.

This abridged report from the Suffolk Chief Constable merely confirmed what was happening in regard to rural policing and what was to become the norm.

Whilst it is appreciated that sensitivity remains in some rural areas, certain factors make it impossible to continue with the village constable policing only his own beat and being available to the public for 24 hours police cover.

Many police problems today transcend the boundaries of village beat areas and mobility and communications, via wireless in police vehicles, are essential to ensure a rapid police response over the whole County throughout the 24 hours each day. The village constable therefore has to take his place in a team to maintain this cover.

Under these necessarily changed circumstances it may be helpful to know the alternative telephone numbers from which police assistance may be sought on the occasions when the local police officer is not available.

Our extensive modern communications network enables us to maintain *constant* police cover by beat patrols, traffic patrols, dog handlers, etc., throughout the whole of the County so that the nearest officer can be directed to wherever assistance is required with a minimum of delay.

From the same issue here are some extracts from the 'Entertainments Report'.

The dances continue to go well and our hall has become a very popular place, particularly for the youngsters on pop nights.

(These were non-ticket, public dances, with rarely any trouble – then)

Coming up there is a play on Friday 19th October by Ipswich Theatre Go Rounds, called 'Gibson's Ghost': watch out for posters and tickets. *(Well, Ibsen is not required reading in West Suffolk).* Also the Horkey will be on 26th October, following on a similar pattern to last year. We would very much like some more people to help entertain and anyone who could do anything, sing, tell stories or jokes, etc. please contact Mr Len Rix in good time.

The last article in this issue helps to paint a little more of the historical canvass of this part of Suffolk. The heading was 'The Fame and Infamy of Some of the Parish Priests of Bygone Stradishall' and was written by K. P. Bland.

The Domesday book written in 1086 tells us that the village of Stradishall possessed a church with 30 acres of land. This early church was probably constructed from wood, for no part of the present building is earlier than 1300. In 1389 a Parish Guild was formed whose function it was to furnish torches in the church in honour of St Mary and St Margaret. Other than this we have very little information about this early period until the reign of Henry VI, when we read that in 1453-4 Wills Aleyn was rector of 'Stradishall' and the following year Robert Goodale succeeded him to the office.

The first rector who achieved any note (or is it notoriety) was William Procter. He succeeded Johannes French to the office in September 1631. A graduate of Oriel College, Oxford (under the name of William Mathew!), it was to Cambridge he went on 12th April 1644 to be tried for 'delinquency' (i.e. neglect of duty) and to be ejected from the rectory. Whether this neglect was directed towards the spiritual needs of the parish we are not told, but in soliciting for the material needs of the church he certainly did not show negligence. In 1638 Richard Wigges, Gentlemen, donated two 12 inch pewter Alms dishes fittingly inscribed 'Remember the Poore'. Two years later the same Gentleman presented the church with a magnificent pair of pewter flagons. All these items still bear witness to the fact that William Procter was rector!

Moving forwards through the list of rectors we come to 1738 and the induction of Patrick Murdock. While in office at Stradishall, Dr Murdock was made a Fellow of the Royal Society (in 1745) and contributed several papers to that Society. Among this rector's many friends was the poet, James Thomson whose most famous work was a long 4 part poem entitled 'The Seasons'. It is said that Thomson wrote the section 'Winter' at Stradishall while staying with Murdock but the lack of rural references makes this doubtful and the more so as 'Winter' was first published in March 1726, long before Dr Murdock moved to Stradishall . . .

December 1973

A profile was published on local tenant farmer John Long. A member of the Parish Council at that time and also Chairman of the Wickhambrook Memorial Social Centre and Chairman of the Community Council, he still represents Wickhambrook on St Edmundsbury Borough Council (Bury St Edmunds) and was its mayor in 1990–92. Sadly, his wife Helen died in 1993.

John Seaber Long was born in Great Wilbraham, Cambridgeshire (14 miles from Wickhambrook), in June 1918, where his father farmed Hall Farm. After leaving school in Cambridge he spent two years in London during which time he worked at Sainsbury's for the princely sum of 25 shillings (£1.25 to you) per week. In July 1939 he was called up for six months training. But as hostilities broke out very shortly after his call-up, he was to spend the next seven years with the Royal Artillery. He was commissioned in 1941, attaining the rank of captain one year later.

Having in the meantime learnt to fly, he was attached to the 661 Air O.P. Squadron RAF Royal Artillery. At the start of the D-Day invasion he went to the Normandy beachhead with the Canadian Army Group RA as one of their four air spotters, and later saw service at Calais, Boulogne and Cap Gris Nez. With the advancing armies he next served on the Leopold Canal in Belgium, at Nijmegen and Arnhem in Holland, finishing up on the Dortmund Ems Canal in Germany.

Following the German surrender he spent the next six months with the Flying Taxi Service for General Horrock's Headquarters Staff and was then transferred to the Agricultural Division of the Military Government in Hanover, and there he stayed for the next two years. He recalls, with some nostalgia, the price of drinks there, remembering particularly that gin was only 3d per double tot.

After his demob in 1946 he married Miss Helen Sutherland, whom he met when stationed in Edinburgh in 1940. The wedding was in St Peter's Church, Edinburgh, the ceremony being conducted by the Dean of Edinburgh. They have two daughters, one living in Canada and the other in Germany where her husband is serving with the BAOR.

On his return to England in 1947 John took up employment as farm manager for Sir Robert Adeane in Babraham (Cambs.) and remained for five years. In 1952 he took over the tenancy of Peacocks

Farm, Farley Green, Wickhambrook, from the late Arthur Worledge and here he and his wife now reside.

In conclusion, it is perhaps of interest to mention that from documents in the family possession the origin of the Long family is Long of Branches Park, Cowlinge, which claims descent from one William Longespee, the only child of a liaison between King Henry II and Fair Rosamond (de Clifford) in 1170–77. William married Ela, Countess of Salisbury, who inherited from her mother one third of the Manor of Cowlinge, which included Branches Park. – *H. L. Gray.*

February–April 1974

Most of us think that the controversy surrounding the election of women priests is an event of the nineties. In fact the Methodist Church admitted women to the Ministry in the early seventies, an issue on which E. S. (Stan) Golding had something to say in a letter to the editor. If Stan Golding can now look down and see how this, and many other reforms, has affected his beloved Anglican Church, he would be making several turns in his grave; if he had not been cremated.

Sir,

The Methodist Church, admitting women to its Ministry, clearly rejects the teaching of Saint Paul:-

Let your women keep silence in the churches; for it is not permitted unto them to speak; but they are commanded to be under obedience, as also saith the law.

And if they will learn anything, let them ask their husbands at home; for it is a shame for women to speak in church. – 1 Cor.14vv 34–35.

Let the woman learn in silence with all subjection.

But I suffer not a woman to teach, not to usurp authority over the man, but to remain in silence. – 1 Timothy 2 v12.

And withall they learn to be idle, wandering about from house to house; and not only idle, but tattlers also and busybodies, speaking of things which they ought not. 1 Timothy 5 v 13.

A woman's place is in the home – not in the pulpit. Let them, therefore do their duty in that state of life unto which it has pleased Almighty God to have called them.　　　　　E. S. Golding.

Stan Golding received his comeuppance in the following issue in three letters from three ladies. Here are two.

Sir,

St Paul, surely the Father of all male chauvinists, would doubtless like Mr Golding have us all 'barefoot, pregnant and in the kitchen ' – or, as Judge Blackstone laid down in the 18th Century:- In marriage husband and wife are one person, and that person is the husband'.

Wake up, Mr Golding – It's 1974!

Yes, Women's Lib!　　　　　Mrs Edna B Cowan

Sir,

Mr Golding criticises the Methodist Church for admitting women to the Ministry and 'so' rejecting the teaching of St Paul. I feel that Mr Golding himself should be glad that over the centuries the Christian Church has constantly re-thought its doctrines and from time to time rejected some. Were this not so I fear that Mr Golding might well find himself suffering one of the more barbaric of the church's punishments for the heresy contained in his letter. In his last paragraph Mr Golding indicates that St Paul is synonymous with Almighty God. Men and Women have been burned at the stake for lesser heresies than this.

May I also add that if God has placed women permanently in 'the home', he has also given men bows and arrows, fur loin cloths and asked them to be the killers of animals. Only a man who has stuck to this traditional sex role can in any honesty criticise any woman or man who has progressed beyond this stage.   Janet Baker

In the Community Council News report in the same issue came a paragraph that indicated that the previously highly successful public dances were now attracting troublemakers.

Shelves were to be put up around the Social Centre Main Hall to try and reduce the mess on dance nights by people breaking glasses on the floor.

Further on, someone signing himself as 'Sturgeon' had this to say:

It is disquieting to see how the road and lanes of Wickhambrook are becoming afflicted by that urban menace, litter – broken bottles, beer cans. In some parts of the village there are so many cigarette packets and plastic containers on each verge and in each ditch that it is hard to say anything to a litter lout. With some justice he asks: 'Why pick on me, mate?'

June 74

The then Editor, the Rev. Reeder, gave a further example of the growth of vandalism in the village. However, visitors we had from London almost fell about laughing that such an incident could even make the pages of a local magazine.

People using the phone box at Thornes Corner are often put at great inconvenience because the directory is often in tatters and sometimes it has disappeared altogether.

The Post Mistress says that in 18 months she had replaced six directories and all have disappeared! Windows too have been broken and on one occasion the apparatus damaged.

An anonymous contributor wrote of his/her 'Nostalgia for Ponds', and deplored their disappearance.

How gradual has been the disappearance of so many village and farm ponds over the last 50 years. Machines have taken over the work of horses, the milkman's bottle from the cow and the disappearance of sheep. Without their demands the ponds fall into disuse and gradually become redundant and overgrown. To extend adjacent fields they have been cleared, drained, filled and ploughed over. The remaining animals usually drink from a piped water supply as do we humans. This has been a slow process, and as vital in the loss of habitat for wild life as the loss suffered by the increasing persecution from our modern farming practices. Increasing human population with its demands also takes a serious toll.

Wickhambrook has no communal village pond left on any of the eleven village greens. The last was at Attleton Green and in a very sorry state until recently infilled and the small area cleared by the Council *(With a more enlightened Council the small pond has since made a comeback)*.

On the farms that have ponds and rivers the effect of pollution from modern fertilizers is severe and has a disastrous effect on the aquatic life. How sad it is to walk along the banks of our small streams and find so few ducks. The semi-tame mallard fights a losing battle against the gunman and may disappear all too soon. Seldom are teal, widgeon, tufted, pochard and shoveller duck seen unless one travels to areas of special conservation, and how few gunmen would recognise them and hold their fire if perchance the odd pair flew within range.

On the following page was a report of the formation of the Wickhambrook Clay Shooting Club. Shooting at clays may have taken some of the danger away for the few surviving wild duck, but today they are even rarer, apart from the ubiquitous mallard.

President of the Clay Shooting Club was John Long, with most members of the Claydon family serving on the Committee.

JOHN OF LYDGATE – RAGS TO RICHES

A short article in this same issue from a Mr A. Webb revealed a little more of the depth of history of West Suffolk, on this occasion in the adjoining village of Lidgate.

In about 1370 a boy was born at Lydgate who was to become a renowned poet, achieving a position equivalent to that of a modern 'poet Laureate' at the court of Henry V. He was John Lydgate (or John of Lydgate), known to his contemporaries as 'the Monk of Bury', having been admitted to the Benedictine Monastery at Bury St Edmunds at the age of fifteen.

In his own time he was greatly esteemed, and some regarded him as the equal of Chaucer. Later ages have been less kind; he has been described as 'a prosaic and drivelling monk' and 'as removed from Chaucer as far as the East is from the West'. Whether his poems were good or bad he wrote a lot of them; over two hundred totalling about 140,000 lines. The best, by common consent, is 'London Lickpenny', the saga of a countryman who travels to London where he finds lack of money a distinct disadvantage (possibly the title was a mediaeval misprint for 'Lackpenny').

He died about 1450. His house still stands in Lidgate. He seems to have been one of the wealthier inhabitants, though said to have been, in his boyhood, an 'ordinary urchin'. A true story of rags to riches.

August 1974

In the Community Council report the first news was given of the plan to build a village swimming pool.

It was proposed, seconded and approved by the meeting that the new committee appoints a sub-committee at its first meeting to look into the possibility of having a village swimming pool. It should be emphasised that the pool ought to be positioned near to the school for use of all age groups...

The following were elected on to the Community Council Committee: Mr Addison, Mrs Alexander, Mr Bayman, Mr Bean, Mr Cook, Mrs Crysell, Mr Crysell, Mrs Forsyth, Mr Hampshire, Mrs Hampshire, Mr Hicks, Mrs Jolland, Mrs E. Jolly, Mrs O. Jolly, Mrs Jones, Mrs Lawrence, Mr Long, Mrs Long, Mr Mortlock, Mr Nunn, Mrs J. Read, Mr Reed, Mr Reeder, Mr Rix, Mrs Stivens, Mr Turner and Mrs Webb.

Nineteen of these twenty-seven were Suffolk born.

Towards the end of the report it stated:

Mr Len Rix told the meeting that Country and Western dances do not appear to be the money raiser that Pop Groups and Discotheques are. Regretfully there will be less of them in future.

October 1974

Extracts from the report of the Cricket Club, who had won seven of their games during the season.

A cup competition was held during the season in which Gazeley, Whepstead and Stansfield were invited to enter. Gazeley won the Cup this year and Wickhambrook were runners up.

On Bank Holiday Monday the Plumber's Arms annual pram race raised £18 for the club in spite of the bad weather. During the afternoon a cricket match was held between the Greyhound and the Plumber's Arms.

Then the following intriguing item perhaps indicated that some players had spent too long in their respective pubs beforehand.

The Cricket Club would also like to express their sympathy to those who received minor injuries during tea on August Bank Holiday Monday.

January 1975

*Further indications that the Horkey – whose origins go back
several hundred years as a post harvest party for the farm workers
and their families – was losing its appeal appeared in this
Community Council report.*

There was some criticism of the group at the last cabaret, who could
have been more versatile. Also, the conjuror at the Horkey was too
late in the evening and too long, and there seemed to be children
everywhere. As the Horkey is a family affair it was felt little could
be done *(!)*. Any suggestion of stopping children would stop mums
and dads as well. More entertainment, or 'gob stoppers', might
help. An Olde Tyme Music Hall was to be arranged for the New
Year.

April 1975

*Peter Bayman, Secretary of the Community Council, announced
in this issue that the Reverend Donald Reeder had had to give up
the editorship of 'The Scene' due to ill health. He offered a warm
welcome to the new editor, John Bean. Further in his report
he stated:*

Some people were offended by the Olde Tyme Music Hall but the
majority seemed satisfied. The contents and type of material were as
much a surprise to the Entertainments Committee as they were to
the audience.

*Some of the jokes and antics were pure Anglo Saxon bawdiness
and were not appreciated by some of the stricter non-conformist
members of the audience.*

Significantly, the secretary's report ended with this statement:

'ADMISSION TO ALL DANCES MUST BE BY TICKET ONLY'

*The writing had been on the wall for some time and the message
fully understood when considerable rural mayhem occurred at two
consecutive public dances. 'The lads' from Bury had turned up
to fight 'the lads' from Haverhill, using Wickhambrook hall as
an away ground and the hall furniture for weapons.*

*Billy Underwood had been telling people in The Cloak that he
was sure that some of the vegetables being exhibited at the
flower show had not been grown in the gardens of Wickhambrook,
but purchased in Bury market. We persuaded him to write to 'The
Scene' about it.*

I have lived in Wickhambrook for nearly 50 years and I have seen a
lot of changes, some for the better and some for the worse. When
we had our flower show committee meetings it used to be a happy
family. Now it is more of a business, and not so interesting to me
now.

When people entered things into the show in the past, there used
to be two members of the committee who would go round to see that

you actually had that thing in your garden. Nowadays you can show anything in the show, which I think tends to spoil it.

June 1975

HARD OLD DAYS

This was my second issue as 'Scene' editor. Not having seen some of the earlier issues published before we arrived in Wickhambrook, I did not realise that my next door neighbour Mrs Edith Claydon, matriarch of the Claydon family, had already been 'profiled'. Fortunately, she did not enlighten me, because in the event her story supplemented her first interview and painted a broad picture of 'Wickhambrook Life in the Twenties'.

Fifty years ago life in Wickhambrook obviously had its charms. But if for some it was the 'good old days', it was also 'very hard old days' compared with today. At least that is the impression we gained when your editor talked to Mrs Edith Claydon.

Mrs Claydon, who was born in Dalham and came to live in Wickhambrook in 1920, states that one of the main differences compared with today is the state of the roads. All the minor roads and what we now call 'B' roads were merely dressed with stones, and road menders could be seen trundling their wheelbarrows to fill in the numerous holes with stones. The main Bury to Haverhill road had superior treatment however, for here a steamroller was used to bed the stones down more firmly. There were very few cars about until the Thirties arrived. One of the first people in the village to possess a car was Dr Wilkin, which replaced his pony and trap.

At this point Mrs Claydon added that the late Dr Wilkin was also the only doctor and that in those days you went to him if you were really sick and 'not just for a cut finger'.

If you wanted to go shopping in Bury St Edmunds or Newmarket you went by bicycle or pony and trap, if you were fortunate enough to have either. If not, you could either go on Mr Ernie Hurrell's old bus on market days, or with the late Mr Charlie Cook of the Duddery, who had a horse drawn van fitted with seats and some sort of shelter if it rained. Eastern Counties did not start their bus service until the Thirties.

In those days Wickhambrook was served by five pubs. In addition to The Cloak, the Greyhound and the Plumber's Arms (still with us today your editor is pleased to say), there was also the White Horse, which closed down about 1926 and is now where Dr Batt lives, and the Walnut Tree at Attleton Green, now the home of Mr & Mrs Crysell. The Walnut Tree was also known as the 'Sizzle'. This was because the landlord, the son of a butcher, invariably had either some sausages or chops cooking in a pan on an open fire for the customers. The Walnut Tree only closed down some ten years ago.

The Cloak was an independent pub – the others all being Greene King – where the landlord, Mr Ted Mills, brewed his own beer for sale to the customers. It was bought out by Greene King when Mr Mills died in the Thirties.

Opening times would be around 9.00 a.m. right through to 10.00 p.m. There were no saloon bars or bars as we know them, just a tap room, and they were, of course, lit by oil lamps. Mrs Claydon stated that with Friday being pay day, some – certainly not all – of the old boys would be in the pub all day on Saturday while their wives waited hoping that there would be some money left to buy food with at the shop – which stayed open to 9.00 p.m. for this purpose. Less timorous wives would go into the pub and pull their spouses out if it seemed to be getting too late!

In the homes everybody relied on wells or pumps, and some even ponds, for their water supplies. Mains water, as with electricity, did not come to Wickhambrook until the mid-Fifties. Only the large houses had indoor sanitation.

The use of slates was still common at Wickhambrook School in the Twenties and there were no school dinners or free transport for the children. Those children who could not get home to their dinner would bring what their parents could afford, often a piece of bread and dripping, and would wash this down with a drink of water from an old enamelled mug which used to hang on the side of the school pump. The toilets were primitive and heating was provided by coke stoves. School leaving age was thirteen.

On the Land

Mrs Claydon points out that as opposed to today, even on the smaller farms there would be eight or nine men working (twelve hours a day) during harvest time. The most advanced equipment was the self-binder which tied the cut corn into sheaves which were then put into shocks (known as stooks in other parts of the country) by the men. There was an art in building a good shock which meant that even in heavy rain only the outside sheaves got wet. Boys would often be employed for leading the horses and as they moved the carts away they would shout 'Hol'on' and the man on top of the cart would thrust his fork into the sheaves to hold them firm.

Many women, together with their children, would get permission to go gleaning and would often pick up as much corn to produce a sack of flour – the corn was taken up to the mill for grinding.

The straw in those days was good for thatching because it was not broken up as with a modern combine.

Two great visual differences on the land in the Twenties was that although a number of tractors were being used, the use of horses still dominated up to the mid-thirties, and there were, of course, far more hedges. The removal of hedges to make bigger fields did not start until after the last war. Another noticeable difference was that every farm kept some cattle. This was useful for the villagers who, in the absence of milk-roundsmen as we know today, would call at the farm with their jugs for their milk.

Growing of sugar beet was well established in West Suffolk by the Twenties and Mrs Claydon states that she can remember as a girl at Dalham the excitement in the village when some Flemish farmers arrived just before the First World War to show local farmers the best way to grow sugar beet.

Social Life

There was no Wickhambrook village hall in those days and the only meeting place for social evenings would be in the pubs. Harvest Horkeys were organised by individual farms.

The Women's Institute started in Wickhambrook in 1926 and Mrs Claydon was one of the founder members. They used to meet in the school room until they raised the funds to build their own hall in the mid-Thirties. The hall was also used for weddings and many other functions.

There was no sports ground either. Mrs Claydon's husband, the late Mr Tom Claydon, was a keen athlete and on Boxing Day morning 1920 he organised the first local football match in Pump Close meadow, then at the top end of Grove Farm. Mr Claydon then spoke to Mr Fass, who at that time was the owner of Giffords Hall, who agreed that if Mr Tom Claydon could find a piece of land for recreation purposes he would pay for it.

Some land used as allotment plots was purchased in 1922 and is where the recreation ground and Memorial Social Centre stands today. Dr Wilkin gave a cup for the football competition and Mr Fass gave a shield – the Fass Charity Shield – which is still played for today.

In the same issue a sign of the times was the announcement confirming that dances in the village hall could no longer be open to the public because of violence. The editorial stated:

... Readers will see from the reports of the Community Council meetings that the income gained each month is, on average, considerably lower than what it was a year ago. The major reason is, of course, due to the fact that non-ticket, 'open' pop dances have had to be discontinued due to troublemakers from outside the village. With ticket only dances attendances tend to be lower.

August 1975

*My editorial reported on the success of the Carnival and Flower
Show, It's a Knockout and the Week of Activities, July 5th–12th.*
... but only one sour note to spoil the proceedings. This was the
cancellation of the Car Treasure Hunt, due to the objections made
to the police by one woman who lived near but not on the route.
The lady, who admitted that in her younger days she participated in
car rallies (a better class of people in those days!), had retired to this
area from London for peace and quiet and apparently her objection
to the rally was that it might frighten her cats.

To express a personal opinion, this is just the attitude that makes
Suffolk born people suspicious of 'townies' who come to live here;
treating this unrivalled country area as something for their personal
convenience rather than a community where the interests of everybody must be considered. Conversely, it also gives the opportunity
to point out that those 'ex-townies' who do offer their help in a
community spirit should not be accused of 'trying to take over the
village'. This is not a personal moan, as your editor is thick-skinned.

*It was also reported that a new ambitious project to aid the
school was now under way.*
As we go to press Mrs Hampshire of the Swimming Pool Fund
informs us that she has now had a letter from the Education Authorities giving their approval to go-ahead in the collection of funds for
the Wickhambrook Swimming Pool project.

*Among the 'Letters to the Editor' there was this from an
American Air Force family.*
In a few weeks we shall be returning to the United States after four
enjoyable years in Wickhambrook. In saying good-bye to the many
friends we have made in the village during that time we would like in
particular to thank everyone for their kindness towards our children:
Timothy, Teresa and Tina.

We are sure everyone will agree that there is no place like home.
But if you have to spend four years away from it then you would be
hard pushed to find somewhere better than Wickhambrook.
Yours faithfully,
Sonja and Ted Sessums

*On the following page we were informed that young Tim
Sessums had in fact won that year's Snooker Cup. In the
knock-out competition organised by the local club in the
Memorial Hall he beat Ken Parker in the semi-final and Alan
Hinds in the final.*

*A more serious matter was the report from the Parish Council
on their meeting with three members of St Edmundsbury
Council Planning Department in attendance. Not for the first
time, or the last, pressure was being exerted on Wickhambrook
to drop its resistance to expansion.*

Mr Casson (of the Planning Dept.) said he was surprised that the Parish Council was not happy about the layout of these proposed houses. He understood that the main objection was to terraced planning. The Government was short of money and so it was a saving to have terraced building and to have as many houses as possible on a given area. The houses, he said, were for all people, not just the people of Wickhambrook. Parish Councillors all expressed their opinion against this terraced building spoiling a rural area and even suggested that as finances were low it might be a good idea to defer the building of these houses. Mr John Long said he felt there were too many to one plot. Another Parish Councillor attacked the idea as 'a daisy chain of bungalows'.

The last Councillor was almost certainly long-serving and local born Vic Harrod and well known for speaking his mind.

Unfortunately he died as these 'Chronicles' were being prepared.

Jean Coe, then secretary of the Playgroup, reported:

The pre-school playgroup continues to meet every Tuesday, Thursday and Friday morning. The meetings may not be exciting news material, but they seem to be enjoyed by all.

The highlight of last term was a visit to Colchester Zoo on June 17th. A count of heads revealed the same number returning as made the outward journey and we have not heard of any violent character changes, so we assume we brought the right people back.

October 1975

A belated report on the Cricket Club's fortunes over the season appeared. This year they had won ten out of 22 games. As with nearly all other reports at that time, people did not have christian names (or even forenames), only initials.

Whepstead and Wickhambrook reached the final this year having defeated five teams on the way, including last year's cup winners, Gazeley. Whepstead batted first and scored 125 runs in 20 overs. Wickhambrook seemed to have quite a task to beat that score, particularly as the first 7 overs showed a rather low score. But P. Stiven and G. Steggles then formed an impressive partnership in the batting, and Wickhambrook went on to win with 131 runs off 18 overs. P. Stiven batted throughout the entire game scoring 68 runs and M. Prigg finished the game with flourishing style, hitting a six!

December 1975

Remembrance Sunday

What a pity it is to my mind that no wreath was placed on our War Memorial in the Wickhambrook Cemetery this year or last. There were just four little crosses, three of them placed by one of the poppy sellers who has done this job for over 30 years and one by a couple who always remember a relative killed in the Second World War.

The Royal British Legion does a very good job in remembering old comrades who made the supreme sacrifice and also those disabled as a result of two wars and in arranging district services. But how nice it would be if we as parishioners made up our minds that there should be a service around our memorial and a wreath placed on it every Armistic Sunday.   *A. C. (Alf) Hicks*

February 1976

Feeling that I had established myself as the 'Scene' editor, I thought I would use the occasion of deep drifting in heavy January snow falls as an opportunity to express my opinions on the removal of hedgerows. Particularly as in this area fewer hedgerows had been removed than in Cambridgeshire and Mid-Suffolk; so there was at least something to preserve.

PLEASE LET'S KEEP OUR LAST FEW HEDGEROWS

The heavy snowstorms at the end of January proved one thing for me: the value of hedgerows in preventing heavy drifts. It was very significant that wherever there was heavy drifting, which cut the road from Wickhambrook to Bury in six places, for example, it was always at a point where the hedgerows had been removed. No doubt the farmers and farmworkers who read these words are thinking 'Ah, here we go again, somebody else to have a dig and tell us how to run our farms'. This is not my intention, for I am the first to recognise that farming is the most efficient 'industry' in the country today and that it is unmatched by anything on the Continent and unsurpassed by any country, including the USA. Also, it would be ridiculous to imagine that modern farming machinery, which gets more complex each year, could operate in the little pocket handkerchief fields, each surrounded by its own thick hedge, that existed before the war.

No, our point is that whilst there must be access and turning points for such machines as harvesters, why can't we retain the hedges along the road sides? Many of these main hedges that still exist have been part of the East Anglian landscape since Saxon times. That is for over a thousand years! Yet there are those, who in order to make another 13 pence an acre profit, would like to rip the lot out and turn this part of the country into a prairie.

Mark you, in dry conditions and high winds there are some places, and not more than ten miles from Wickhambrook, where semi-prairie and dust bowl conditions are already nearly with us. One must assume that it is only when their valuable top soil finally blows into the North Sea that they will at last wake up to what is really happening.

The destruction of the hedgerows has also led to the virtual extinction of many species of birds, and other wildlife, who nest and feed there, coupled with the other hazard they face when insect life, on which many birds feed, is annually exterminated by stubble burning. Apart from anything else, the birds them come into my garden in ever increasing flocks to feed!

However, to return to a serious note, I know from personal conversation that the majority of people who read these pages would ask all farmers and landowners to think very carefully of everything that is involved before they remove our last few hedgerows.

April 1976

I was not surprised to find that my editorial in the previous issue on saving our remaining hedgerows drew some heavy fire from Peter Bayman. We accepted his argument that absence of hedgerows was not necessarily the cause of snow drifts and was pleased to note that he was one farmer whose hedge removal activities had been minimal.

HEDGEROWS AND CODSWALLOP

I must reply to the Editorial in the last 'Scene'. What a load of codswallop!! Snow is the worst disruptor of communications, a fact that we must accept irrespective of the time of day or night it comes or the amount of men and equipment available. I remember in 1962–63 winter the road between where Stan Golding lives and Shadlows being filled up. Not so much because of the absence of a roadside hedge but because the wind and snow were blowing across the road, which is lower than the field and soon filled. The road between my farm entrance and Hall Hill was blocked the same winter. Once again the wind was blowing from the north from the pylon, across the road and the 12 inch bank/kerb with the hedge and ditch on the other side were sufficient to trap the snow. The same thing happened where Mr Jamerson used to live and Joe Tabraham's Cottage. Hedges both sides of the road!! My own drive was blocked in the January this year. The wind and snow blowing through the hedge slowed the snow down and it settled. I am sure we all have memories of roads being blocked.

The point I am making is that when the wind and snow come together the slightest obstacle is sufficient for it to settle. Given these conditions as we had on the night of January 25th/26th, no amount of equipment can keep our roads clear. I speak with experience as I only managed to clear my drive during the night of January 25th from the farm to the main road to find when I turned round to go home that the first half cleared was already filling up. This is a length of road 200 yards long. Think what it must have been like on the roads from Bury St Edmunds to Newmarket, from Chedburgh to Horseheath, from your homes to the office. An impossible task and no amount of equipment which has to be paid for and manned would have coped. We must accept as ratepayers relying on roads for our

61

jobs that at some times our roads will be blocked and there is little one can do about it.

As most of you will be aware some farmers do have council snow ploughs to assist the authorities. I do not think these farmers remove hedges in order to line their pockets snow clearing. Why do we remove hedges? A good question and difficult to answer. I have removed about 1200 yards of hedge in 20 years out of a total of 10 miles.

Generally they are removed to make larger fields, thus improving the efficiency of field work. There are times when hedges on boundaries are removed or even cut to the ground. This is a little difficult to accept. If the hedge was faced and topped into a box hedge I think we could satisfy most critics . . .

Living in what was once part of the Wickhambrook
Workhouse, and before that the House of Correction, my wife and
I found Stan Golding's 'Other Days' column in this issue of
particular interest.

House of Correction, Wickhambrook, 1789.

Joseph Button to take of the parish, Sarah Simmonds, from Easter 1789 – Easter 1790, at 1/- per week and find her in desent clothing and leave her as he find her.

T. Webb, Overseer

Workhouse Account, Wickhambrook 1821

57lbs pork	£1. 8.6.	45 Gals beer	15.2
379lbs cheese	£4.14.9	4 qts milk	4
77 bushels coal	£5. 2.6	4 lbs butter	3.6
2lbs candles	1.4	6 lbs tea	2.7½
10½lbs beef	5.6	2 lbs sugar	1.4

1811

Jeffrey King, £2 in arrears of maintenance, sentenced to 3 months hard labour.

Elsewhere, Lesley Hampshire of the Swimming Pool
Committee reported that funds raised now came to £1500.

June 1976

The Fuller family of Genesis Green, Wickhambrook, reported
on their first year of 'hard labour' to establish a vineyard.

We are most grateful to the voluntary pickers for our first harvest in October 1975, the fruits of which are a special quality Riesling type wine of the Spätlese class. It has been a long hard struggle but now well worthwhile to see the result in the wine, though we have a long way to go before we can expect any monetary profit.

It is a well known fact that the more northerly one can manage to grow white wine grapes satisfactorily the higher the quality should be. So far, practically all the vineyards that have been re-established in these islands are situated in England as the climate is more suitable in the south and south east. East Anglia, because of its many hours of sunshine, is fairly popular and there are quite a number in the area.

Although the Genesis Green vineyard still nominally exists, sadly it never really took off commercially.

August 1976

This was my comment, as editor, on what was probably the most entertaining Carnival day to be held in Wickhambrook, and certainly has not been bettered since.

The Wickhambrook Flower Show and Carnival day may not be the greatest show on earth, but according to some of the professionals who attended the Show on July 10th it was 'the best show that we have seen around the country to be put on by a village.' This comment came from Mr Tim Cody, of Cody's Wild West Rodeo Show – one of the events of the afternoon, and was echoed by the hot air balloonist, who unfortunately found that the air surrounding his balloon was already too hot on that splendid day to allow the balloon to ascend.

With the stunt flyer, the Great Cornard and Sudbury drum majorettes, the side shows, the fair, and the 'It's a Knock-out' between the three pubs, readers may well ask 'what do we do for an encore when next year's show day comes round?'

The centrepiece of the It's a Knock-out equipment was a 30 ft high tower, whose construction was masterminded by John Crysell, a leading village carpenter. From its top, the competing teams slid down a shoot, in varying states of disarray, into a portable swimming pool. The Cloak team were once again the winners, which the then landlord, Eric Seaman, celebrated by sliding down the shoot, champagne glass in hand, bow tie slightly askew – and despite the handicap of being nearer sixty than fifty.

December 1976

Rearrangements in the cemetery inspire philosophical comment from the editor.

In a report on a recent Parish Council meeting it was stated that consideration was being given to the removal of some more of the grave stones from the cemetery – we assume to make it look more tidy. From talking to a number of people it would appear that I am not the only one who thinks that this is wrong, assuming the inscriptions on the grave stones are still legible and have not disappeared through the ravages of time.

Those names in the cemetery are a direct link with the village's past and are names still carried by many people in the area. We can quite understand our worthy councillors' desire to see the place tidy, but where such headstones have fallen over why not follow the example of some of the City of London's ancient churchyards? Here they have placed the headstones round the perimeter, for all to see, and made a small garden area of the original cemetery, equipped with seats so that people can sit in quiet.

Everytime a decision is made to pull down ancient buildings, drop historical names for some of our counties and replace them with some bastardisation of a name (as happened to about one seventh of England recently), pour scorn upon some of our old customs, or remove grave stones, and all in the name of progress, then it is another cut severing us from our past. 'So what?', you say. Well, some of us believe that if we lose all knowledge of our past then for sure we will have no idea where our future lies.

In E. S. (Stanley) Golding's 'Other Days' column we are given the findings of some of his latest researches on Wickhambrook and surrounding villages.

Lidgate 1814.

The poor of this small parish, in number 217, were plentifully regaled on roast and boiled beef, lamb, mutton and plum puddings, on Friday last, by a subscription headed by the Rev. J. Solsen, George Pawsey Esq., and others. – Bury and Norwich Post

Wickhambrook 1763.

Mark Last named by Ann Southgate as putative father of her child, born in the poor-house.

Cowlinge, September 1891

    Buried: Minnie Lucy Littlechild, 13 years
             Mabel Grace, 19 days
             Archibald George, 25 days
             Harriet Eleana, 10 years
             Emma Maria, 5 years
             Frank Theodore, 2 years

Carrying Darwinism to the extreme, ignoring the hit and miss factor of 19th century disease, and writing with 85 years behind him, Stan Golding added this footnote:

Good old days? Yes, of course they were; the strong survived and the weak perished. Why preserve the unfit?

No doubt Stan intended to shock; particularly those with a hygienically packaged concept of Victorian rural life.

Further on in this issue we learnt that the Football Club in its first season in Division One of the Halstead League had had a successful start, winning six of their first nine fixtures and were at present holding third position in the league.

February 1977

Apparently my comments on the gravestones issue had not met with the approval of some of our parish councillors. A report on the Parish Council meeting of January 21st stated:
There was considerable discussion regarding an article on gravestones in the Wickhambrook Scene. It was felt that there was some misunderstanding regarding this matter as to the Council's intentions and it was agreed that a letter be sent to the Editor.

With the prison about to open for custom, this was also on the Council meeting agenda.
Mr John Long expressed grave concern that it appeared there would be no audible warning should a prisoner escape from High Point when the Prison started functioning early this year. It was very much our business to try and allay the fears of those living alone.

The Parish Council report also informed us that it had been very busy in connection with the Queen's Silver Jubilee celebrations due on June 7th.
A committee was formed under the chairmanship of Mr P. A. Bayman and the auspices of the Parish Council with representation of the 20 or so organisations in the village. This has already met and decided to have a door-to-door collection aiming at a target of £1500.

The four main suggestions under consideration as a means of celebrating the jubilee are:

A changing room for the swimming pool (when completed); coppice of trees; a meal and 25 pence piece for all children 0–16 years on June 7th, 1977. As time is short it was proposed, seconded and agreed that 400 25p pieces be ordered in plastic covers. A child survey will be carried out later on.

Another anniversary commented upon in this issue was the 50th Anniversary of the Wickhambrook Women's Institute. This report came from Maggie Thearle, wife of Fred the postman, and now deceased.

Fog Lifts On The WI!

We ended the year 1976 with our 50th Anniversary party. The sub-committee for this event had worked very hard with all the preparations and were at last able to relax and know that everything had been covered.

Come the day and lo! the fog descended. Panic stations, frantic phone calls; the entertainers were held up by fog and were unlikely to arrive that evening. Hasty preparations were made for party games; pencils, paper, balloons, etc. were hurriedly assembled. Then the thought came to us, no entertainers due to bad weather, probably no caterers either. What to do now? How were we going to feed our members and our guests? Well we should have to make do with cups of weak tea and biscuits.

However, the fates were kind to us, for the fog suddenly lifted and all was well. The caterers arrived with their delicious food. Our guest of honour, Mrs B. Ruffell, Chairman of Suffolk West Federation of Women's Institutes, arrived and we were all delighted to be honoured with her presence. Later, to our relief, the merry band of entertainers arrived.

Six founder members were present, Mrs Batt, Mrs Elsie Cook, Mrs Claydon, Mrs Woolard, Mrs Hicks and Mrs Sherman. They were all presented with a small gift in recognition of a half-century membership of the WI. Mrs Batt made a short speech telling us how the Institute started in 1926, and how it has developed since then.

April 1977

Further discussion is published on the plans to celebrate the Queen's Silver Jubilee, and Peter Bayman reports that the Community Council is now ten years old. Its work is appreciated in a letter from Mrs M. Y. Fuller of the Genesis Green vineyard.
Dear Mr Bean,

I am full of admiration for all the work done by yourself, the Community Council, the Parish Council and all the other societies here in Wickhambrook. I think it is sad that in so many other European countries so little is done for the people in villages by their own efforts. And nothing done for the old folk like our 'Happy Hours' Club. I was quite impressed when I gave a talk to them on our vineyard and so glad to see that so many things were arranged for them. When one thinks that millions of old people in other countries have nothing like this, apart from their pensions.

The real point of my letter is to suggest that in honour of the Queen's Jubilee all the older residents, and the older the better, should be asked if they will write down their memories of life as they knew it when young in the Wickhambrook area, which could include Ousden. The more they mention particular places and people and their trade or business, the better. It would be most interesting to have a book made up of these details.

I can remember thinking after reading Mrs Fuller's letter: 'Yes, I must try and find time to do that one day'.

June 1977

Things are going well with the Swimming Pool Committee and Lesley Hampshire reports 'The Big Splash-in Approaches'. Many individuals, clubs and associations – including £350 from the Community Council, and small businesses had donated money and local contractor David Rowlinson had levelled the site with his JCB, F.O.C.

To read Jack Mortlock's contribution in this issue needed some concentration. He had written it as Suffolk dialect is pronounced, and I was told by 'a couple of old bouyes' that he was fairly accurate.

GEORGE REMINISCES

Recently I've spent quite a lot of time in the company of my friend George, who's helped and advised me on my garden. Now George knows a lot about gardens and the land generally having been on farms all his life. 'Wucked over thuty year with hosses – and twenty with they old tractors'.

George is always cheerful (often breaks into song, usually old tunes with his own words – after two bottles of beer there's no stopping him). He's resourceful, can always find the answer to a breakdown. His methods of repair are often crude but usually effective. 'Marvellous what you can due with a hammer and a coupla three niles bor – or a bit of wire or an old bitta tin'. He's as honest as the day is long, has an earthy sense of humour and is superstitious. If George forgets something he never goes back for it, 'bad luck bor', and believes that accidents and misfortunes 'ollus go in threes bor'.

He tells me 'I warnt born about here. I was born up the fen country, that's why I've got webbed fit. I moved to Stansful when I was a little old mite a bouyee. I daint dew a lot of schoolin – I warnt a mucher at head wuck. I grew up into a tidy sized old bouyee and like the others started looking around for an old maurther. There was a nice old gal over Posinfud sort of took me fancy, and I used to go to see she. She ollus dolled harself up, put powder on and had her hair all crimped.

'When I went to see she I ollus cleaned me shews, put on a clean shut and me blew suit. I remember one dark old night arter I'd been over to see she, I thowt I'd take a short cut hum. So I cut acrawse an old midder – garder hell bor it was as black as yer hat, dew yew know? I tripped over suffin in the dark. Dew yer know what that wer bor? It was an old cow lying down. That holly scared me – I slipped in the ditch trying to git back on the wrod. I was a tidy sight when I got hum I can tell yer – wet threw, me shut ganzi and blew trousers darbed upper slud. Made me wonder if she was wuth it.

'I've done every job on the farm. When we were throshing I used to bag the corn on the front of the drum. If you got to walk twenty or thuty yards and then goo up ten or a dozen granary steps haps seventy or aighty times a day with a coombe of corn on yer back, thats eighteen ston bor, you know you ave done a day's wuck.

'Course the wust old job when you are sheening is at the back end of the drum – gitting the chaff and the cave-ins away. That's holly dusty work. But you gotta keep a gooin else you and the drum git choked.

'I remember one time I was wucking on a grut old fild over stonny lay country – four hosses on an old crab harrar – some people call

67

em A harrer's. I just forgit how long agoo that were, tidy while back, late May or early June, and there were a storm. Garder hell bor, I never see weather like it in all me natural. It snew hailstones as big as golf balls – rined holly poring.

Course I could'nt leave the old hosses, so I got wet threw agin.

'Well I shall hadda goo. So long old met.'   *Jack Mortlock.*

VISIT TO THE FLOWER SHOW – AND THE NEWMARKET PREACHER
In the June 1977 issue Mr M. J. Mott of Lidgate gave further recollections of his childhood years during the First World War: this time centred round a visit to the Wickhambrook flower show and fair.

One of my earliest recollections of Wickhambrook was being taken to the flower show 60 odd years ago from where we lived in Lidgate. It was held that year at Boyden End, in the meadow between Boyden Lane and Bunters Road. The gardens of the little row of cottages by the farmhouse were a mass of colour. The old people were sitting by their front doors in the cool of the evening. At least I thought they were old. What on earth were they sitting at home for with all this excitement going on?

I could hear the steam organs, playing tunes of that time. One I remember well: 'We all go the same way home'! I had just started school in Lidgate, we sometimes sang it coming home from school.

My Mother did not seem to be in any hurry, and bided awhile chatting. I think she knew the people, as she sometimes attended chapel at Wickhambrook, or maybe as we were very poor she was waiting for admission prices to drop. They usually did after 6 o'clock.

I wandered across and peered through the railings at the big house at Boyden End. It was much the same as it is today. Opposite was a pretty little garden with a well in it with a little green gate under an arch of rambling roses. There were peonies and pampas grass and flowering shrubs. It is all gone now. The place was owned or occupied by Mr John Frost. They had a little old fashioned one horse shay. I remember well Mrs Frost, who was left a widow, going to Chapel in it, the black horse being driven by her groom-gardener James Edgeley. They sat in the little carriage side by side, no overhead cover, except a big umbrella when wet. Mr Edgeley would help her out of the carriage, see her to the chapel door, go back and take the horse to a stall by the Sunday schoolroom, cover up the shay, and take his seat in the chapel in time for the service. To us lads it looked a good, well ordered way of life. Unlike today's rat race.

Having at last arrived at the show, we looked around at the exhibits, but I was anxious to be watching the fair. I enjoyed the music, the shouting, the shooting and throwing. The ringing of the bell with the big hammer. Young men showing off. Taking off their jackets, making a lot of fuss, and sending the striker only halfway up. While others who did not seem to try, rang the bell every time.

When we went home it was getting dusk and chilly. The old people were still sitting out, maybe they had been to the show earlier and were sitting on their prize money.

A few years later I went to Wickhambrook again, to the little general shop kept by Ernest Hurrell. He also did a stint around the villages with a little horse drawn cart, selling all things, from sweets to paraffin (burning oil). My mission that day was for a gallon of paraffin and a ha'porth of sweets. In the garden in front of the shop stood a fine little statuette, a boy having his earholes washed out with 'Pears Soap'. It amazed me that anyone could so well portray an every day occurrence like this. My mother often did it to the boys, usually with carbolic soap. The statuette was there up till a few years ago. I know not what became of it.

Mr Hurrell even in those far off days had a treasured store of antiques. I looked round the shed where he stored his paraffin. The things he had there were not all bygones then, but he was collecting against the day they would be. I was talking at his back door – years later, when I saw some bottles that were used for mineral waters, with a glass marble. 'Those are not bygones' I said. 'Oh no' said he, 'And how many have you got' 'None', I answered, 'but I can soon find plenty'. He offered me a shilling each for all I could bring him but they had all disappeared.

Most of my happiest associations with Wickhambrook were centered around the chapels. We attended the Sunday School at the lower chapel, and made some life-long friends. A tea-meeting used to be held on Good Friday, which to us children could only compare with Christmas or the school treat. After tea a service of song. A story would be read from the pulpit, and appropriate singing by a practised choir at intervals during the story. These journeys to the meeting are remembered by the cold winds, and the gathering of wind blown anenomes, growing in the lane hedge bottom. The fragile flowers would be forgotten long before we dawdled our way to chapel.

There was the Sunday School treat at Badmondisfield Hall, with rides through the countryside and trips round the moat in a boat called 'Golden Days'. All very simple, but with happy memories.

Many men who preached there were often local farm workers, who toiled in the field all week, and enjoyed the Sunday rest, but some walked miles to preach at other village's chapels. People in Wickhambrook, Ousden and Lidgate will remember a sad faced little man who cycled from Newmarket. Often the weather was bad, the roads were rough and muddy, he would bump along, the rough roads almost putting out his tiny oil lamp. He would preach morning and afternoon at Wickhambrook and finishing up in either Lidgate or

Ousden chapels. He could preach a very good sermon, without notes, and over a closed Bible.

One day my mother took my brother and me to Newmarket station to meet an aunt. The Preacher was sitting in the sun dozing, with a basket of oranges and apples. He would tour the platform when trains came in, selling his fruit – where today not even British Rail can make a living. My mother bought two apples, and offered him the coppers. He patted her hand and said: 'Keep it, thy need is greater than mine.'

And now in conclusion. A few years ago the late Miss H. M. Hurrell sent a message to me, asking if I would come and tidy her garden. Her eyesight was failing. I think she just wanted to see me. Over many years I had known her and her father, and once did a painting for them on a water tank in the yard. It is a very old garden, and I was always reminded of Pip who was called to play in Miss Haversham's garden in 'Great Expectations'. It was always dull on the few evenings I worked there. There was always something eerie about the place, as if it belonged completely to 'long ago'. It may have been the 'Air of Antiquity' statues about the place. Or possibly the fact that in the meantime Miss Hurrell had died, whilst I worked there.

M. J. Mott, 6 Orchard Close, Lidgate.

August 1977

POOL IN – PAVILION NEXT!

The editor's column noted that the Queen's Jubilee celebrations were 'a great success', due to the work of the village 'activists'. It concluded with good wishes to John and Lesley Hampshire who were leaving the village for the Isle of Wight.

Most readers will appreciate the work that Lesley Hampshire has done in helping to turn the idea of the swimming pool into a reality: Yes, it's even got water in it! Well done Lesley and, of course, the other dedicated workers of the Swimming Pool Committee.

In the previous issue Bill Underwood, Wickhambrook Football Team's longest serving and most belligerently enthusiastic supporter, had written in to complain that the teams had to change into their kit behind the back of the hall. He had pointed out that the original plan for the Memorial Village Hall had included a pavilion, but as there was not enough money at the time it was to be the next thing to be built. Bill's letter produced this portentous reply:

In reply to Mr G. W. Underwood's letter I would point out that the Community Council discussed the contents at some length at its June meeting. We agreed unanimously that a committee from the various organisations be set up to look into our possible requirements and improvements and to draw up plans. It was felt that the Parish Council ought to take the lead and were to be written to.

The Parish Council met on the 6th July . . . and agreed unanimously to take the lead and write to all organisations asking them to appoint one representative with a substitute. The first meeting of this committee will be on Wednesday, 2nd November 1977.

Yours sincerely,
P. A. Bayman,
Hon. Secretary the Community Council. Chairman the Parish Council.

October 1977

Stan Golding gives us the results of his latest researches in Bury St Edmunds Records Office: this time mainly based on census returns in nearby villages. With the references to the Mortlocks it is more than likely that he was trying to find if there were one or two born on the wrong side of the blanket. This would give Stanley something to attempt to bait Jack with at lunchtimes down The Cloak.

Hundon Census, 1841.

James Mortlock (35) Not born in this parish, but in Ireland, Scotland, Wales, or some other foreign part.

  Elizabeth Mortlock (32) Born Elizabeth Taylor.
  James (10) Jack Mortlock's grandfather.
  John (5)

Cloak Public House Wickhambrook, 1871.

  Eliza Mills (36) Beerseller.
  Henry (8), William (6), Sarah (5),
  Edward Moses (3)

Hundon Burial, 1750.

  Albertus Halls, struck dead by lightning.

Great Bradley, 1703.

  An infant, left in church overnight, baptised Mary.

Shipping Records, 1848.

The 'Francis Ridley' left London for Australia. Among the passengers were two emigrants from Cowlinge, Robert Eagle (15), farm labourer, employed by James Malcolm of Melbourn, at £18 per annum with rations. William Beavis (15), engaged by Josiah Beavis, on a wage of £16 per annum with rations.

Robert was the second of two illegitimate children born to Hannah, daughter of John Eagle, postmaster and farmer of Cowlinge. John, himself was a direct descendant of William, 'sonne of William Egle and Methusula, his wife, baptised (at Hawkedon) ye xxixth. daye of Julye, 1632'.

Ousden, 1761

A vagrant known as Gypsy Dick found dead in parish, buried.

December 1977

If urban readers think that from the picture painted so far the normal atmosphere at Community Council Committee meetings was of arcadian tranquillity, this was far from the truth. Just take this opening paragraph from the Secretary's report for the October meeting.

Following a remark about the recent losses at some of the dances, a discussion took place. One problem, and perhaps the fundamental one, is that the Community Council and Entertainments Committee are not pulling together. A lack of support from committee members in helping to sell tickets and run events was mentioned. Critical remarks made by some members about types of dances, bands and groups did not help. Close booking and frequency of outside dances were also problems. Accusations, denials and counter accusations were also fired. A fairly long airing of members problems, complaints, criticisms and general dissatisfaction resulted with but a few positive answers.

In a more placid vein, Clive Blanchard, the School Headmaster, appealed for support to celebrate the School's forthcoming centenary.

The Foster Education Act of 1870 saw the establishment of the basic education system as we know it today. It provided for a School Board empowered to levy a rate, finance the buying of land, the building of a school and the appointment of a headteacher and staff.

The Wickhambrook School Board met for the first time in 1875 and after some initial difficulties, bought the present site and opened a school in 1878. Incidentally the total cost of school and school house was £2,200!

A 1978 Centenary Committee is to be set up to organise the activities that are planned but there will be news sheets and posters advertising events. An exhibition is planned for the week 29th May to 2nd June and this will form the central part of the year's activities. It will be designed to reflect the last 100 years of Wickhambrook history with the school as a central theme. Like all the proposed activities I want to involve the community as much as possible and ask for your support, especially for this major event, when I hope to borrow from you any photographs or items that reflect these 100 years of change. Original school documents are to be borrowed from the Public Record Office and I am already accumulating relevant material at school.

February 1978

The Parish Council was assessing public reaction to the idea of using prisoners from Highpoint Prison to work in the village.
... One matter which has caused a lot of debate is the question of employing parties of prisoners in the village. A public meeting was

called, hoping people would attend and express their views. The Governor, Mr Jack Shulman, once again kindly came along to answer any questions, but we only had 25 present out of an electorate of over 750. The meeting passed a motion proposed by Mr P. Rodwell, that its wish was that prisoners should not be allowed to work in Wickhambrook.

It was agreed that the Parish Council should decide whether to employ prisoners in the Churchyard and Cemetery.

What were still comparatively minor acts of vandalism to that experienced in the cities had now spread to the WI Hall, and prompted this request from Mrs Maggie Thearle.

Will the person who took the outside handle off the rear door of the WI Hall please let me have their name and address and I will see that he receives the other half, as half a handle is no good to us.

April 1978

The Community Council Secretary reported that the dance held in the hall to the music, for the first time in Wickhambrook, of a West Indian Steel Band had been a great success. No comment on this new event from the editor, who was taken up in riding his hobby horse along the remaining hedgerows.

. . . When you drive around East Anglia generally it is soon apparent that most places are far more affected on this score than Wickhambrook. At least our farmers set an example by keeping boundary hedges.

It is not just a question of the hedgerows, but also trees, whether as copses or as boundary rows, that are being depleted faster than new ones are being planted. The devastation of Dutch elm disease is, of course, the main culprit here.

June 1978

We reported with enthusiasm a musical evening that was held in the Parish Church. Many thought it might become a regular feature. Alas it was not to be – although, later on, Karaoke night did catch on.

It never fails to amaze me that Wickhambrook can offer a variety of organisations and social events – ranging from play groups to 'gentlemen's' stag nights – that are frequently not matched by towns with twenty times the population.

This thought again came to mind following the concert of music for strings, directed by Professor Yfrah Neaman, which was held in the Parish Church on June 3rd by courtesy of a most enthusiastic Rev. Bill Davis. The concert was part of the Wickhambrook School Centenary and Mr C. Blanshard, the headmaster, pointed out that it was hoped that the profits from the evening would go to purchase some musical instruments for our local children.

Our thanks go to Professor Neaman (who lives in Wickhambrook) for the excellent performance that he inspired from his thirteen pupils, past and present, from the Guildhall School of Music in London. The quality of the performance coupled with the environment of our church on a summer's evening made it a memorable evening for the 150 audience present.

Talking to two of the musicians after the concert over a glass, or two, of an excellent medium dry white wine provided by the Fullers from our local vineyard at Genesis Green, it was a pleasure to hear how much the musicians enjoyed playing for us. They said that they found the audience response, coupled with the surroundings, more exhilarating than playing at the Festival Hall!

Further on the Secretary's report showed that music tastes were still healthily mixed in Wickhambrook, with a Country and Western band being booked to round off the Flower Show and Carnival Day.

His report also stated:

... The pop dance and discotheque held recently was a great success, not only because it was well supported but because a good profit will be made of around £85. Although it was successful we are not going to fall into the trap as before of holding them regularly and often. For those who may not know, we ran into 'trouble' at one of these functions a couple of years back. But for some long, hard and pleading talks with the police we would have been banned from getting a licence with all that that implies.

For his 'Other Days' column we managed to persuade Stan Golding to confine his researches to the history of the Wickhambrook School, in view of its centenary. The Edgeleys, the family with the longest unbroken residence in Wickhambrook – going back four centuries – were well represented.

Wickhambrook Elementary School.

A School Board was established in 1875, presided over by the Rev. J. D. Hulls. W. C. Fuller appointed clerk, at a salary of £12 per annum.

The school was built for the accommodation of 240 children and opened in 1878. William Brown was Head Teacher, a post he retained until 1922, and the Rev. A. J. McKechnie Chairman of the Board.

At a Board Meeting in 1878 it was unanimously agreed that children not belonging to agricultural labourers should pay 4d. per week.

Log Book Entries, 1897.

January: Ally (sic) Edgeley, living at Mole Hill, reported to be suffering from diphtheria.

February: The Edgeleys returned after 5 weeks absence from diphtheria.

These were the children of James Edgeley and his wife, Betsy Jane (Shafe). James will be remembered by many old residents as 'Squaddy Jim', a shoemaker. All children, according to the late 90-years old Annie Maria, were born in the old workhouse, their father having inherited the leasehold of the property from his father, Charles Edgeley. Charles was a direct descendant of Henry Edgely and his wife, Elizabeth (c1625–1701).

Althea ('Ally'), Jane and Clara (twins).

Major *(This was his Christian name, not his rank)* Gascoign (Killed in France May 1917).

Adolphus (Having emigrated to Australia, he was killed at Gallipoli in 1915).

Harold (Ashes scattered at Attleton Green).

Annie Maria, born 31st December, 1884.

Extracts from Log Book.

1898 September: Attendance throughout the week very poor, the principal cause being 'gleaning'.

1900 Holiday today (2nd March) given in honour of the relief of Ladysmith.

1915 A Zeppelin passed over the village.

1927 Essays in connection with the Empire Day Medal Association were judged by Miss McKechnie. Medals were presented to the following children:

Bronze: Norton Hicks and Elsie Loynes

Aluminium: Stephen Bradfield, Victor Harrod, James Edgeley, Joyce Holden, Gladys Wallage, Brenda Cant.

October 1978

ELEVEN LOCAL INNS AND COMMON ALE HOUSES

Jack Mortlock was in form again with an historical review of the many 'Local Inns and Common Ale Houses' that once existed in the area. One suspects that his tale was slightly embellished.

Back in the last century and in the early part of this one the local people were well supplied with 'Pubs'. There were no less than eleven, possibly more. Some of them were fairly large providing food, lodgings and stabling for horses. Others much more modest, with perhaps a single room of the house for drinking.

These smaller places and possibly some of the larger ones, were started when it became known that a man could make a good drop of home brew and was willing to let others come to his place and pay a penny or tuppence a pint to drink it. This was before licensing hours were introduced during the First World War.

Until that time it was possible to drink at any hour. Beer was served in earthenware pint pots. Those richer or higher up the social scale often had quart jugs with a couple of glasses. There were spittoons around the room and sawdust on the floors to soak up spillage – and for those who missed the spittoons.

A rather unhygienic custom that persisted among the older generation up until the Second World War was to hand your pint pot to a friend or two, the first to 'take the top off' the second 'to have a wet' before drinking it yourself.

This custom is reckoned to go back to the days when someone may have tampered with the drink to do one a mischief or even to poison.

The Black Horse at Farley Green, always known as the 'Bluster' on the boundary between Wickhambrook and Stradishall.

Much used by Gypsies and diddi-coys; many a 'shady' deal in broken winded horses, lurcher dogs and game took place. A long high-backed wooden seat known as a 'settle' was in the passage way by the back door, usually occupied by the women and children, who were not allowed to get mixed up in the deals and fights that took place in the bar. The owner of the place, the Squire of Stradishall, closed it down after the First War, because of its reputation and the amount of game that was being poached from his land. It was later a bakery and now a private home.

The Walnut Tree at Attleton Green was always known as the 'Sizzle'.

There are two explanations for this title. One that the seisal plant for making rope grew nearby. The other, and more likely, was that the landlord was a butcher, fond of eating well and often had a pan of homemade pork sausages sizzling in a pan on the hob.

Some older readers who can remember back fifty years or more will recall that several of the Sizzle regulars were known by nicknames only. Squibby who lived in an old caravan nearby, Old Waters, Benzoo, Towser, Nabs, Cobbler Billie and Tooty Foot were just a few. The pub was closed after the Second War and is now an attractive private home.

The Greyhound at Nunnery Green, still going well. It was originally a thatched house. The Green family took it over in the early twenties and had family connections with it until quite recently.

The Queens Head beyond Genesis Green, always known as the Wickham Queen.

The landlord had a business as a carrier taking goods and passengers to Newmarket twice a week. Until its closure it was kept by the Stittle family. It is now a private home.

The Rose and Crown Hotel at Malting End was one of the larger pubs and always referred to as the Crown.

It was closed before the beginning of the century. It had food and lodgings and cart and horse accommodation – the writer occupies what was once the ostler's cottage.

Almost opposite on the corner of the main road and Wash Lane stood a Malting Shed, hence Malting End.

The Cloak still going well, and the only pub called 'Cloak' in the country. *(For full historical details see Jack Mortlock's report from September 1989).*

The White Horse opposite the church, now the doctor's home and surgery – closed in the early twenties.

It is said that the landlord on holidays or festive occasions employed a man to lead or wheelbarrow the drunks to the triangle of grass at the entrance to Wash Lane and to leave them until they recovered. It is reputed that a tunnel used to lead from the White Horse under the road to the rectory. The writer made a point a few years ago of being there when the sewers were being laid deep in the road, but no tunnel appeared.

The Plumbers Arms Commercial Hotel. The boundary of Denston and Wickhambrook goes through the property.

In the old days it catered for horse drawn travellers with accommodations for people, horses and carts. A guest book going back to the 1800s is owned by a friend of mine in the village.

The Red House closed many years ago – now a private residence and headquarters of J. Marshall the transport company.

Reputedly a 'rum old place', sometimes referred to as the 'Blood Tub' – you could, I understand, get a pint of strong beer and a 'thick ear' for tuppence. Maybe you still can??

The Depot at Ashfield Green a thatched house just before Aldersfield Hall. A beer house and coal merchants. Closed many years ago.

The Black Horse the last house in Wickhambrook on the Hargrave Road – now a fruit farm. Just remembered as a pub by the older inhabitants.

December 1978

Clive Blanshard, the School Headmaster, thanked the village for their support for the centenary celebrations.

... The active support the school enjoyed was especially rewarding because it came from so many people, who gave so generously. Alf Hicks and the Centenary Committee, the Managers, parents, children, Professor Neaman and his brilliant students, but most of all, people from the village. Your support was especially appreciated at the time of the exhibition when we were willingly loaned items of incalculable worth and interest. Equally well supported of course were the sales, the dance, the concert, the balloon race, the tree planting ceremony and the thanksgiving service ... And don't forget the SWIMMING POOL (can we ever, did I hear someone say?). Surely a happy coincidence that the pool was opened this year.

Following Jack Mortlock's dissertation in the previous issue on the history of the pubs in Wickhambrook and district, Alf Hicks gave some of his recollections under a heading 'The Man Down the Well'.

Together with many others I was very interested in Jack Mortlock's account of the local inns and common ale houses that existed at one time in Wickhambrook. He seems to have done his home work very well and stirred our memories.

I can remember my grandmother complaining bitterly about the Greyhound. She could see it from her cottage at Nunnery Green and would watch my grandfather on his way to work!? If he got past the Greyhound she heaved a sigh of relief, but if he went in – well, he was there for the day. She used to say: 'I wish that Greyhound would fly afire!'. But when council houses were built she complained because she could no longer see it! Incidentally, the only photograph of my grandfather she had was him sitting down leaning on a barrel marked XXX !

The Red House, Bury Road used to be quite a meeting place for bricklayers etc, my father was one. I remember him telling the tale of working on a well bricking the inside at Gatesbury Farm some distance from the 'Reddy', as they called this inn (The Red House). The well fortunately was dry. The late Walter Gumwood was at the bottom of the well when they decided to pull the chain up and leave him there. The rest of the gang, including my father, went off and spent several hours drinking at The Redhouse before returning to draw Walter up. They acclaimed it a huge joke – what Walter thought is another matter!

February 1979

THE DAYS OF LAYED-BACK BANKING

H. J. Mott of Lidgate told us of the layed-back banking facilities, now long since gone, that existed in Wickhambrook up to the early fifties.

Just after the Second World War, I received a cheque from the 'War Agricultural Committee'. It was a resettlement grant to help restart my small business, which I had lost through my call up.

I knew nothing of banking. It was a Barclay cheque, so I took it to their branch in Bury. A very haughty girl bank attendant said: 'Have you an account with us?' The answer being no: 'You can't cash it then, you must open an account', she said and turned to attend to another customer. Confused, I left the bank and decided to go and see my one time Sunday school teacher, Clem Fuller, who managed a small branch of Lloyds Bank in Wickhambrook. I explained my errand. 'Why certainly', he said. 'Much handier, bless my soul, you don't want to go running into Bury every five minutes'.

Having opened the account, it was some time before I again visited the bank. It was a Friday morning, the bank was open chiefly for farmers to collect wages etc. I knocked at the heavy door and waited. I could hear voices, and thought it improper to walk in unbidden. A burly farmer came along with a black retriever. He gave the dog a gentle prod with the stick he carried, and commanded it to 'sit'. The dog obeyed, he gave a nod to me and opened the door and walked in. After a time I knocked again. A chorus of voices said come in.

Round the room in comfortable chairs sat half-a-dozen farmers. This was not my style, each could witness the other's business. My business was quite trivial. I had a fifteen pound cheque to deposit and I required most of it back in ready cash.

Justin Brooke sat smiling, with a twelve pound chip basket on his lap, filled to over-flowing with bank notes. I was not worried to do my small amount of business in front of him. He was very broad minded about money. I had worked for him for six years in my early twenties.

Mr Fuller sat at a large square dining table. He seemed to close his mind against the chatter around him. In spite of the exacting business of handling and counting other people's money, he still carried on a limited conversation.

A huge potato was lying on the window-sill. 'Anyone like to guess the weight of the potato?', he said. 'Brought in by a customer yesterday'. Being a careful man, he quickly added: 'No prize for the winner'.

A little further money-grubbing, and he turned to me. 'How is the painting going?', and to the assembly: 'Mr Mott is an artist you know. Had a write up in the "East Anglian" and the "Bury Free Press"'.

After a bit more counting: 'Oh yes, it's all in the papers', as though it were an occurrence of world wide importance. It did something, however, to restore my confidence.

I once took a pound note to the bank. A mouse had eaten a hole in the middle. I was given a long form to fill in. I expected a refund straight away. 'My dear man', said Mr Fuller, 'the bank could not do that'.

I asked again weeks later, but nothing yet. I was annoyed. 'They're a frightened lot', I said, 'this bank of yours, I've seen men die for less'. He was very hurt. 'Come, come', he said, 'you must not speak of the bank like that', as if it were blasphemy.

Mr Fuller had other irons in his fire; he did insurance and was manager of some local schools. He could be seen cycling round on his high bicycle, which he mounted from behind and which had an extended wheel nut on the rear. He would place one foot on this, propel himself forward with the other and finally spring on to the saddle. He carried his papers etc. in a large bag suspended from the cross-bar.

In the summer he wore a semi-stiff Panama hat, which in case it should be blown off in the wind, was anchored to his jacket by what looked like a bootlace.

The bank, the post office, the Cloak and Woolards shop were quite a busy part of Wickhambrook. Only the Cloak remains.

On the 'Readers' Viewpoints' page, Bill Underwood reopens the controversy on the moving of headstones in the Church (the old) Cemetery.

Dear Sir,

How many people in Wickhambrook have had a recent look at our Old Cemetery? How many are aware thất headstones marking the graves of their forebears have been removed? The headstone of my Uncle Wiliam Cook (known whilst he was alive as Cobbler Billy) disappeared some time during the period 14th–21st December, 1978.

I doubt if this can be attributed to vandals since similar headstones disappeared in the same period. Also, we are paying a substantial village rate mainly to keep the Old Cemetery up to a standard. A man is employed to maintain it. I have not seen any sign of improvement. Has anyone else?

These are the questions for the Parish Council. To what extent are they observing the wishes of the older inhabitants of the village as regards the last resting place of their forebears? And are they satisfied that money – our money – spent by them is justified by the results?

Yours faithfully,
(Bill Underwood)

April 1979

Writing as a Parish Councillor, Alf Hicks replied to Bill Underwood's letter on the headstones in the old cemetery.

I am sorry that the headstone of his Uncle William (a man I remember very well) has disappeared. A few others have too, and I hope they will be found.

'No sign of improvement in the cemetery maintenance!' Bill, I am surprised you should say this. There is a great improvement: graves levelled, etc and there will be more improvement. Dead elms are to come down and the path will be cleared of weeds. The Chapel is to be repaired – and soon.

A final comment. I remember 'Cobbler Billy' having as his assistant another local character, Humphrey Thorogood, known as 'Towser'. They kept the cemetery very well by hand!

THE HAMLET BY THE BROOK

Having a couple of pages to fill in this issue I gave readers some of my thoughts on how Wickhambrook may have got its name.

An interest of mine for a number of years is the study, in a rather amateurish way, of the origin of place names in Britain, and England in particular. Reading a recent book by Dr Margaret Gelling on 'Signposts to the Past: Place-names and the History of England', I was most interested to see her comments on place names of the Wickham/Wycombe variety. Their sites have been plotted and they seem to stem from the Latin word *vicus* (in Medieval Old English 'v' became 'w'), which was the term for the smallest unit of self-government in the Roman Empire. Dr Gelling goes on to say that there are indications that this name survived in Old English as a description of a Roman town that had not been swamped by Germanic settlers (i.e. the Angles and Saxons and later the Vikings).

Imagine, it is probable that Roman Legionaries stood guard in Wickhambrook 1800 years ago and perhaps a retired Centurion, after many years on Hadrian's Wall, established a small villa in the 'small settled place by the brook'! Conjecture, maybe: but after all the remains of a Roman villa can still be found at Lidgate. Also, Stradishall derives its name from Strada, the Italian word derived from the Roman Latin for 'street', and there is evidence that a Roman road went through that area. Worth considering is that one of the nearest parts of Wickhambrook to Stradishall is called Wickham Street.

In regard to the comment by Dr Gelling on places in England that were not completely swamped by the Angles, Jutes and Saxons from 450–600 AD, from another source I read that Walsham-le-Willows (in Suffolk) got its name from the Anglo-Saxons (the 'le' bit coming in later from the Normans) as an area where the 'Welsh' lived among the Willows. The Anglo-Saxons called all the Celtish British stock 'Welsh' and even today an old-fashioned German word for a foreigner is 'Waelsch'.

Coming back to Wickhambrook, in another reference book in Bury records office one will see that Attleton Green is Anglo-Saxon in origin and was originally Atta's Ton. 'Ton' is the Saxon word for a homestead. So that was where a Saxon, or more likely an Angle in these parts, set up his homestead.

In regard to place names deriving from a person, as in Atta's Ton, Haverhill is supposed to stem from a Saxon or Angle called Hafer who set up his encampment on the hill there. The same Hafer in the sixth century is reputed to have led his men right across England, driving the 'Waelsch' before him until he reached modern-day Pembrokeshire in West Wales and set up a camp by a river ford, now known as Haverford West.

As many readers will, of course, know, the Angles not only gave East Anglia its name but gave England its name: the land of the Angles or Engles. They came from what is now the borderlands between Germany and Denmark. Those who settled in the North part of East Anglia became known as the Northfolk (Norfolk) and those in the South the Southfolk (Suffolk). Their racial kinsmen, the Saxons, who came from farther south in Saxony, established themselves in Essex – the land of the East Saxons. Also, Sussex – the land of the South Saxons; Middlesex – the land of the Middle Saxons; and Wessex – the West Saxons.

So next time our MPs decide to get rid of some ancient county or borough name, let us remind them that they are helping to destroy the evidence of our origins, of *our* 'roots'.

In a subsequent letter to 'The Scene' Alf Hicks made it clear that he did not think much of the suggestion that Wickhambrook could have had Roman origins. He, and others, stayed with the Wick-ham-brook: a hamlet by a brook (ours is a tributary of the River Stour) and where the 'wick' stood for 'boundary'.

June 1979

The editorial was headed 'Thoughts Whilst Waiting For Summer': thoughts highlighting the disadvantages as well as advantages of the country dweller.

Living in the country we are far more concerned – and obviously affected – by the weather than the towns folk; not least because many are dependent on the vagaries of the weather for their living. In consequence, after the winter we have been through we have all been looking forward to the return of the summer sun. At the time of writing, we have only seen it for four days in Mid-May and for three hours last Sunday!

Then we have the crippling cost of petrol, which hits East Anglia worse than London or other big cities – and yet we are the people who are far more dependent on cars for transport to work, shopping, etc. On top of that, the average wage is one of the lowest in the country. Our MPs, whether for East Anglian seats or other country areas cannot do a lot for us because they are swamped by the MPs for the cities and suburban areas – and what makes it worse is that in East Anglia we are only allowed one MP for every 90,000 voters, whereas the average city and town MP is elected by only 45,000 voters!

Yet in spite of all this, East Anglia has the fastest growing population in the whole of Britain whilst the cities continue to shrink in population (certainly of 'original' inhabitants).

The answer is the value of life that you get, its closeness to nature, and the community spirit, personified here in Wickhambrook in particular during the past winter. It might be sunnier in California or Spain, petrol and food might be marginally cheaper in London or Birmingham, but it is that indefinable quality of 'community', of 'belonging', that makes those who come to Wickhambrook rarely wish to return to the city.

There have been several boundary changes since 1979 that, on

82

each occasion, have helped to redress the difference in population sizes of country and inner city parliamentary seats. But with the continued drift from the cities the country folk are always under represented in varying degrees.

In the June issue's report from the Community Council, the secretary was concerned about 'mischievousness and even vandalism' in the Memorial Social Centre following a Junior Youth Club night. Bob Everitt, Youth Club organiser, apologised for the trouble with a plea: 'More Helpers Needed'.

The issue of public footpaths dominated the annual Parish Council meeting. Forty-seven local Rights of Way were listed.

At the annual Parish Meeting those present were able to study the Footpaths Map provided by the Suffolk County Council, and to hear the statement giving details of all Public Rights of Way in Wickhambrook.

All the paths shown on the map will be walked, and their condition noted. We hope all landowners will co-operate. Suitable volunteers are needed to help check our paths – please contact the Clerk.

Anyone who thinks the map or statement is in any way wrong is asked to let us know.

Horses are only allowed on bridleways or byways, not on footpaths.

August 1979

Alf Hicks reported:

The closing of the Undertaking business of A. Bailey & Sons is regretted in the village and a tribute should be paid to Leonard, Lewis and Eric Bailey for the way in which they have conducted this business over many years, proving very helpful and sympathetic to a vast number of people on very sad occasions. The Bailey's are, of course, still carrying on their building business.

October 1979

It was the end of the then customary stubble burning season, which used to lead to many hedgerow fires and the occasional thatched house fire. An article was published on the role of the Wickhambrook Fire Station, that still exists adjacent to Justin Brooke's fruit farm at Clopton Hall.

... Small towns and villages are often protected by part-time firemen, more correctly called retained firemen. Wickhambrook is one of these small communities where the prohibitive cost of wholetime professional fire crews means that a retained station is the only economic way that a fire service can be provided to cover the area. However, this in no way infers that the service received by such areas is in any way second rate. Indeed, retained and wholetime firemen work side by side . . .

The firemen of Wickhambrook, and all other retained firemen for that matter, are drawn from all walks of life, each being employed outside the fire service in some normal civilian occupation. However, they are available throughout the day and, indeed, the night to answer emergency calls, which are signalled by the small radio bleeper constantly carried by each man. A retained station such as Wickhambrook has a complement of approximately 12 officers and men. The station operates as a self-contained unit within the Suffolk Fire Services 'B' Division, which is administered from Bury St Edmunds.

. . . Each year the fire engine and its equipment is used by the Wickhambrook firemen at some 75–85 calls in their own and adjoining areas.

Appropriate with this report was a notice that the Community Council was again putting on its first class fireworks display at the rec on November 5th. Until 1992, this was reckoned to be the best village display in West Suffolk. The Parish Council report ended with this paragraph:

A parishioner had expressed deep concern at the attitude of farmers burning straw and causing houses to be filled with smuts, and paint and linen getting soiled. Was there not some code of conduct by farmers over straw burning and could not some warning be given to house holders in the vicinity?

Steve Taylor, who in later years was elected as a Parish Councillor, had a short letter published. It caused considerable comment.

Rumour has it that the 3.69 acre field between Thorns Corner and the school was sold for about £11,000. If correct, then this is about twice the current price for agricultural land hereabouts. So what highly profitable crop is to be planted in that field?

Perhaps we should all look into it – while we can still look beyond it!

December 1979

A VISIT FROM PRINCESS ANNE

It was reported that on the afternoon of November 5th, prior to the bonfire and fireworks, Princess Anne descended upon the village by helicopter and was received by Peter Bayman as the Parish Council Chairman. She had come to visit the Hill View Riding School for the Disabled.

In the Community Council News section, in spite of the hard work put in by Bob Everitt and other helpers the Youth Club came in for another panning.

...Now we come to another problem area – the Youth Club. It is quite obvious to us and the MSC (Hall) Committee that there is an increasing amount of damage to the centre which if it continues and can be attributed to the Youth Club will result in one of two actions.

Firstly to close the club, which will be a pity. But as the young will soon realise, one of the many facts of life we all unfortunately have to bear is that the majority suffer because of the minority.

Secondly, to levy the cost of these repairs onto the Club, the monies to be raised by their own efforts and not by hand outs from this committee.

A local born farm worker who I would often talk to in The Cloak was Billy Wright, easily irritated if you addressed him by his nickname of 'Shacker'. Conversation would have to be in the early evening, before Billy's alcoholic intake dulled his brain. Although sometimes incapable of riding his bike home from the pub, he was never ever late for work at Justin Brooke's farm the following morning. He has long since retired, and now props up a corner of The Greyhound.

We were pleased to give Billy the pleasure of seeing himself in print, in 'The Scene'.

Talking to Billy Wright on his birthday last month, he began to recall some of the incidents in Denston and Wickhambrook on birthdays long since past.

For example, on his seventh birthday, in 1929, he recalls that one of his regular jobs after school was to help his father look after the cows at Chantry Farm, Denston, then owned by Mr Charles Hicks. Bill's wage for this help was 1d. an hour.

Another way he had of earning a penny in those early years was to conveniently position himself by the gate at Wickham Street Manor whenever there was going to be a meet for fox hunting. As Lady Briggs came out of the manor on her way to the Sand Pitts, where the foxhounds met, he would smartly open the gate for her and receive a penny. He would do the same for Sir Charles Briggs, but couldn't always guarantee *his* penny!

During our conversation, however, Billy Wright went back several times to a later Saturday morning job he had, which he obviously found the most interesting, when he was nine or ten. This was with Mr George Cook, who had a coal merchants in the Bury Road. They used to go down to Clare Station to collect the coal, with the cart being pulled by a sturdy old horse called Boxer. Bill's job was to hold the bags open whilst the coal was being weighed out.

He recalls that one morning whilst they were doing this the stationmaster came up and said: 'I have a case here for Mr Justin Brooke. Could you get it on?' 'I should think so', said George Cook. 'Come on boy, we ought to be going now we have a tidy old load.'

So off they went, with their normal coal load, plus the case, 'which was none too light'. The case must have pushed old Boxer to the limit, Bill told me, because as they came up the Folly, old Boxer got slower and slower. Mr Cook turned to Bill and said: 'Boy, you had better get off and shove up behind. Every little helps.' And it did and they eventually got to Stradishall, where the coal was delivered at 6d. a half-cwt bag.

After his work, old Boxer would be put away in his stable near the Plumbers Arms and be given a meal of beans. Bill's job here was to get the beans from their pods by thrashing them with a thrail. Bill's wages for the morning were usually two old pence – mark you, he would get quite a few sweets for a ½d at the shop in Denston!

April 1980

WEST SUFFOLK'S FIRST WOMAN DRIVER
Finding that the memoirs of some of the older people of the village made interesting reading for 'The Scene', I interviewed Mrs Dorothy Mills, said to be West Suffolk's first woman driver.
The next time we male drivers resort to muttering 'blooming women drivers' we should spare a thought for West Suffolk's first woman driver, Mrs Dorothy Mills, who today lives at Attleton Green.

Although it is over 65 years since she first came to Suffolk at the age of 16 – to live with her aunt and uncle who ran a Grocer's shop in Clare – she still has a strong Gloucestershire accent from her childhood days spent at Arlingham on the banks of the Severn.

At first, her aunt and uncle sent her for dressmaking lessons. Then in 1914 the First World War began and with men going to the front in ever increasing numbers, her aunt and uncle found it more and more difficult to find drivers for the five horses they used to deliver groceries within 10 miles of Clare. So Dorothy Goulding (as she then was) found herself on the road to Cowlinge or Long Melford delivering groceries by horse and cart.

Late in 1914 the Clare grocers acquired a Model T Ford van for their deliveries: the first such van seen in this area. As two boys could not pick up the knack of driving it, she asked her uncle if she could have a go. Mr Harry Deaks, the Clare coach builder, brought the van along and took her along the Cavendish road, then said 'you steer it', which she did until Cavendish. Then, Mr Deaks told her: 'Right, you drive it to Sudbury'. At Sudbury Mrs Mills was told to park outside a pub, whilst Mr Deaks went in to quench his thirst (and perhaps fortify his courage). She then drove all the way back to Clare, pulling up at the Bell Hotel.

Following three further lessons, Mrs Dorothy Mills went on the rounds for the next seven years. She would crank start the old Model T herself – not bad for a 17-year old girl – and did all the running repairs. Having once watched some mechanics take the head off the engine and carry out a 'de-coke', she decided that she would also do this herself.

It was not long before Dorothy Mills was carrying something far more valuable than groceries in her Model T van: the shell and bullet torn bodies of our wounded soldiers from France who arrived in ambulance trains at Ingham station. Up to three times a week she would join a convoy of ambulances, cars and other vehicles and take the wounded from the station to the Suffolk Red Cross Hospital at Ampton Hall. The seriously wounded stretcher cases would go by ambulance and the walking wounded would go by car or van. She told me: 'The worst thing was to see them coming in suffering from mustard gas burns'.

She was the only woman driver (in reality a 'girl' driver) and would sometimes have to wait at Ingham station until 3.00 a.m. before the train came in. Having taken the wounded to Ampton Hall she would then arrive back at Clare at 6.00 a.m., with only bicycle lamps on the front and candle lanterns tied to the spare wheel at the rear. She recalls battling through several snow drifts and taking more than one skid on the frosty roads – and roads that bear little resemblance to those of today.

It was at the end of the war that she picked up another victim of mustard gas at Ingham station. This was Monty Mills of Wickhambrook.

In 1922 they were married and came to live opposite Woollards Corner, where Monty Mills, being a motor engineer, opened the first Wickhambrook garage. Motor repairs were carried out here and there were also two cars for hire. Mrs Mills recalls often driving the smaller one taking young chaps and their girls to dances.

In 1924 they moved away to Haywards Heath in Sussex, but returned to Wickhambrook fifteen years ago, when her husband tragically died, partly as a result of effects of the gas attack in the First World War.

As I finished my interview, Dorothy Mills with justifiable pride, showed me a commendation she had received from the Suffolk Red Cross. Let it speak for itself:

'The Members of the 41st Detachment, Suffolk Branch, British Red Cross Society, desire to express their thanks to you for the valuable help gratuitously given by providing the means of transport, when they were summoned to render assistance in the removal of the Sick and Wounded arriving at Ingham Station, for the Suffolk Red Cross Hospital at Ampton Hall.

'Of the 92 convoys, bringing 6,568 patients, the Detachment was called on 40 occasions at all hours, and never failed to report on duty.

'We feel that it must have entailed much sacrifice on your part, but at the same time, that it was gladly undertaken with the desires of doing all in your power to help those who were suffering on our behalf.

'We ask you to accept our grateful thanks for the help you thus rendered.'

With no living relatives, Dorothy Mills died alone in Bury St Edmunds hospital in 1987.

Having wrecked a Capri after skidding on black ice and rolling it twice, the resultant broken bones led to my temporary move back to London so that I could carry out client meetings via public transport. This had two effects on 'The Scene'. One was that my interview with Mrs Dorothy Mills was published four months after the event, whilst I was in London. Two, Peter Bayman took over as editor. He wrote in that April issue:

I am pleased to report that John Bean is making satisfactory progress, although I believe his arm is still in plaster. We look forward to seeing him back in the village, particularly me, for once again I am deputising editor.

... I notice in the Community Council News report two 'I-told-you-so' items. One is that the entertainments committee has resigned and is not being replaced and secondly the Senior Youth Club has been closed. Are those the results of the 'old sweats' having had enough?

June 1980

A report from the Wickhambrook Recreational Development Fund showed that it had built up a balance of £1591.85 and, importantly:

Plans for the Pavilion have also been drawn up and finalised and, as of yet, the committee have not reached a final decision as to whether they should organise the building work themselves or employ a builder in this respect.

... The Pavilion will be an extra room at the back of the Memorial Social Centre and will be available for the use of all organisations in the village. Our Committee's aim is not to please a mere twenty-two people in the village, namely the football and cricket teams...

David Green, Secretary

August 1980

Bones mended, I was back in Wickhambrook, and back in the editorial chair.

... As reported elsewhere in this issue, the Flower Show and Carnival was a great success this year. I mention this because an incident occurred on the day that again caused me to reflect on the better quality of life here than in London, where I recently spent four months. A case of vandalism was reported where the two main poles

of the Scouts tent had been purposely broken. It is sickening, absolutely pointless and not to be minimised. But I could not help con-
trasting it with many things I saw when staying in South Woodford
(not a particularly 'tough' area). A classic case was to see two 14-year-
old skin heads walk up to a shop window and just push it in for the
hell of it. Needless to say, nobody did anything. I wasn't going to,
with two broken arms.

December 1980
*Better news from the Youth Club, reports the irrepressible Bob
Everitt.*
We have started the new Youth Club year very well. On the last
count there were 35 members and they all seem to enjoy themselves.
We have now got a football team, so if anybody knows of another
young team that would like a friendly game, would they let me know.

I am sure the older children of the village have heard of the over
15s discos which are organised by a committee of youngsters. Parents
will be pleased to know that there is only a soft drinks bar which
means that they only come for the dancing.

*Elsewhere in 'The Scene' we are told of a farewell night
organised at 'The Cloak' for departing landlord and landlady,
George and Thelma Jarman. The new licencees were Bert Keating
and his wife Rita from Scotland.*

February 1981
*It was announced that Bob Everitt (Youth Club Organiser) had
been appointed Vice Chairman of the Community Council. As the
Secretary put it:*
... whom we shall help, encourage and hassle in his new post according to our varying moods.

*Also announced was that indoor ice skating had come to
Wickhambrook!*
On the 16th (January) ice skating came to Wickhambrook. This idea
of Mr Everitt's brought something very new and almost unthinkable
to the Memorial Social Centre. It was therefore with great interest
that young and not-so-young flocked to the Centre, many having a
go. Although not many 'Cousins' were spotted or flattened to the
walls, this marvellous idea will be repeated to the delight of so many
who thoroughly enjoyed themselves.

*Unfortunately prohibitive costs meant that it was only repeated
once.*

*Further on came more evidence that the days of leaving your
door unlocked had definitely gone.*
The police officer partly responsible for the Wickhambrook area, PC
Abbott, would appreciate the help of the general public in an effort
to combat the villains responsible for recent break-ins and robberies.

This help could be in the shape of taking the numbers of cars parked in unusual places, with the occupants not leaving the vehicle. Also reporting any phone call where the caller did not speak.

The above being of more interest to those living in isolated areas, could affect the safety of property throughout the village . . .

April–June 1981

Stan Golding gave further results of his researches, including unearthing more illegitimate children and the odd case of incest, in his 'Other Days' column in these two issues.

Workhouse Accounts, 1821.

At a Select Vestry meeting it was agreed that inmates of the house be provided with drugget dress, and that all do attend Divine Service on Sundays, accompanied by the master, to keep them orderly. Furthermore, it was resolved that victuals be delivered to persons after they have clean washed their faces and hands and combed their hair.

It was also agreed that Hannah Garrod be permitted to leave the house this day and be allowed to take her wearing apparel, one shift and a spinning wheel, and to have an allowance of 1/- weekly.

John Edgely's wife appealed for her husband to be freed from prison. This would have been his second wife, Jemima Pearson, whom he had married in 1810 following the death of his first wife in 1805, by whom he had had four children. Prior to the second marriage, Jemima had given birth to an illegitimate child in the workhouse, John's brother William said to have been its father. In 1818, John himself had to pay laying-in costs of 2/- weekly in respect of a child born to Martha Rowling. So, by 1821, Jemima would have had nine children to support during her husband's imprisonment. After his release, the couple had four more children, amongst whom was Charles, father of James Edgeley, who will be remembered by some old residents as 'Squaddy Jim' the shoemaker of Mole Hill.

In May 1837 parishioners met for the purpose of signing a request to the Board of Guardians for consent to let the workhouse, which had been sold for £180 by Parish Estates in the April of that year.

In December 1837 the churchwardens and overseers of the poor let the premises, then in possession of a George Peacock, for a period of 19 years at a yearly rent of £10.

Census Returns, 1851

John Edgeley having died in 1846, Jemima was living with her son James, who had married an Ann Taylor, by whom he had six children: Sarah (1839) who married John Claydon; Ann (1841), married to George Challis; Lettice (1835), married to John Hurrell; Mary (1844); Thomas (1847), married without issue.

At this time the family was living at Attleton Green, and Williams

(brother of James) in New England Road. Charles, a half-brother of
James, was still living in Mole Hill.
*(In the September 1984 entry Stan Golding gave the Edgeley's
family tree.)*

WICKHAMBROOK'S MOST FAMOUS SOLDIER
*Stan Golding also submitted his first article on Wickhambrook's
most famous soldier, Thomas Heigham. After notable service
to Queen Elizabeth 1st and James 1st he retired to the family
residence at Giffords Hall, Wickhambrook and was buried in
All Saints Church following his death on 15th August, 1630.*

*An ancestor, Richard Heigham, is traced to Heigham in
Suffolk in 1340, with an earlier Thomas Heigham coming to
'Wykhambrooke' to reside at 'Gyffordes' Hall in 1488.*

*For several years prior to his death, Stan Golding, usually in
company with Herbert Edgeley – the last surviving
Wickhambrook member of the family, would stand in silence by
Thomas Heigham's tomb and pay his respects to the memory
of 'the old soldier'. He was also accompanied on one occasion
by Jack Mortlock, another old soldier, and the author – an
'old sailor' (National Service).*

*Upon the altar tomb rests the recumbent effigy of Thomas
Heigham in armour with sword at his side. On the wall above
is this memorial:*
The worthy and well deserving Souldier, Thomas Heigham, Esquire,
a Gentleman of Antient Descent & noble Allyance, suted to both
with an Heroyall spirit, who, in his younger years entered into the
profession of Armes at the Syete of Nimigen, when Queene Elizabeth, of glorious memory received the Hollanders into her protec-
tion, and when her most sacred M'tie sent over the Earl of Essex
with forces to establish King Henry the 4th of France on his throne.
This Gentleman in the action before the Cyttye of Roan was shotte
with a bullett and maymed, and her M'tie upon just information of
his merits remunerated him with a good Pension and appointed him
to take charge of a Company in Ireland, when Sir William Russell
went over as Lord Deputye. In these wars he is worthy to be
remembered for his good Service: at the taking of Belmay, Elnay
and Skillen and at the Winning of Slage Castell, in Connaugh, and
at the Curlew did brave Service, when some English Commanders
were slayne in the attempt against Claine Castell with much difficulty
and loss of most of his Company he escaped the Eneky's Surprise
and at the overthrow given the Rebellious Irish, assisted by Spanish
Forces at Blackwater, fighting single with Sir Edward Stanley, that
was Commander of some of the tratorous Troopes (and took part
against the Sovereign) gave him the Guerdon of Disloyalty, and
deprived him of Life and Honour.

91

August 1981

The Editor's page commented upon the two 'big days' that had just been held in the village.

The first was, of course, the Flower Show and Carnival and apart from the one heavy shower that nearly sunk the floats en route, it did turn out to be a good day, both for enjoyment and weather.

On that day, July 11th, the country was in a state of shock by the riots that were occurring in many towns and cities. As I looked at our crowd enjoying themselves and our young people in youthful high spirits but causing harm to no one, I again thought how lucky we are, in spite of some disadvantages, of living in this area. As for the causes of the riots, well it is not my place here to discuss them, other than to say there are plenty of young people in our area who are unfortunate enough to be without work, but they do not riot. So draw your own conclusions!

Then we had the Royal Wedding (the Prince and Princess of Wales), with the party for the children and our own 'reception' in the evening. A good time was had by all...

It was a good day and so pleasant to see so many happy faces on the television in contrast to the scenes of late. Even a couple of old 'Cromwellians' that I know, grudgingly admitted that perhaps our system of Monarchy is better than having a President.

The Community Council reported details of its recent AGM.

A resolution was put before the meeting that it endorsed the committee's decision to give financial aid to the Recreational Development Fund and after much discussion and several proposals it was agreed that a sum of £1700 be given in two stage payments, £1000 immediately and the balance when building was under way.

Elsewhere, David Green, secretary of the Recreational Development Fund, wrote:

The first objective of a pavilion looms nearer. It is hoped building will start this year aided by voluntary labour, skilled and unskilled.

...Future plans after the building of the pavilion relate to the development of the six acres below the present recreation fields.

The breezes of change – not quite 'winds' – were also echoed by Derek Pope, Clerk to the Parish Council.

... Strong representations were made to BSE District Council against their decision to sell off the spare land in Nunnery Green/Boyden Close area (opposite the Doctors' Surgery) for further building. They agreed to reconsider the matter, but our latest information is that they are still intent on selling for development. Meanwhile another field is up for sale opposite Meeting Green. We must be vigilant that this is not added to the 'permitted development' area, or we shall cease to be a village and become 'urban sprawl'.

This footnote, under the heading 'Don't Shoot The Singer – Or Her Pheasant' appeared on the last page.

Who was it who shot at the model pheasant on the roof of Diane Solomon's rebuilt and rethatched house?

A good restoration job here after the disastrous fire.

October 1981

Fred the Post (alias Thearle) marked his retirement with an article recounting his experiences over the previous ten years delivering the mail in Wickhambrook and, initially, also Stradishall. At first he doubted whether he had chosen the right vocation for a 55-year old, particularly as he had to be lifted off his bike for the first week.

... Over the years I have made friends of lots of children and seen them grow from toddlers to teenagers. I have befriended most of the cats and dogs, of which there are many, and also learned most of the dogs' names: mainly for my own well-being, for if you call the dog by name he may be less inclined to bite you.

It is the old story of the dog always biting the postman, but I have more trouble with the letterboxes. Some are too small, others have all sorts of things hanging behind them, making it hard to get the mail through. Some have queer flaps (I never found out their exact use) which tend to eject the letters as you let go of them. There is the strangest of all types – a pair of brushes set like teeth in the opening, presumably to polish the mail as it passes through. Others are so near the ground that one would think the postman crawled round: they may in some areas, but not in Wickhambrook.

It has been an interesting and at most times enjoyable ten years, with a few adventures, such as early one morning stopping a runaway horse on Cemetery Hill and wondering what to do with her, with no one in sight. Another time helping to rescue a nun from her over-turned car outside the chapel early one cold morning. And of course one winter's dark morning slipping up outside The Cloak, of all places. I thought I had broken all my ribs, but I only managed bruises and within two weeks I was back spreading the good news.

Fred Thearle's successor was Colin Bird, who became an active member of the Community Council, then a Parish Councillor, an inspiration (to a few an irritant) to the yearly Pantomime, and is still ensuring that the mail goes through.

December 1981

Some of the findings of a survey in Wickhambrook conducted by student doctors was published.

1. If you took a random sample of 100 people in Great Britain you would expect to find that age groups were like this:

Age 0–15 years	16–44	45–64	65+
25	38	23	14

In Wickhambrook we have a higher proportion of older people. Our figures would be like this:

Age 0–15 years	16–44	45–64	65+
20	34	20	26

2. In the census people are divided into 'social classes' according to the jobs they do. In Wickhambrook we have:
Slightly less Class I than the national average.
More than twice as many Class II.
Many fewer Class III.
More than the usual numbers of Classes IV and V.

It is unlikely that this situation has altered radically over the last 13 years. It shows that Wickhambrook residents are either comfortably well off, which includes many newcomers – who can afford to buy property – or poorer than most townsfolk and unable to buy property. Unfortunately, the latter are often the genuine locals. They are lucky if they can find council property to rent.

February 1982

The Editor offers thanks to the snow clearers.
As I write it is hard to imagine that we were covered with snow almost continually for over six weeks, and with heavy drifts before Christmas that cut many of us off. As several of our readers have pointed out, we must thank the farmers and other individuals that we were in the main not cut-off for more than 24 hours in most cases – others being marooned for up to three days. They came out with their tractors, put in many hours and burnt up many gallons of fuel, so that we could get about our business. And for this they do not even receive one penny towards the cost of the fuel, let alone anything for the wear and tear on their equipment. The Government's cut-backs have stopped local authorities giving farmers, or others, some compensation towards their fuel and labour costs in snow clearances. Anyway, many thanks to Peter Bayman, John Long, Jeff and Frank Claydon, John Marshall, Justin Brooke Ltd, Mr & Mrs Gardner (Giffords Hall), David Midwood, Michael Read, Tom Shepherd, Tom Bradfield, Frank Fearnley and Norman Debenham. If we have missed anybody out, our apologies for doing so.

April 1982

Sue Allen reports on the February meeting of the WI.
Mr David Lee gave us a brief history of Justin Brooke Ltd followed by three of his pre-war films, made by Justin Brooke himself.
Those of us who are newcomers found these a fascinating glimpse of the recent history of our village; whilst the members who are 'natives' enjoyed spotting friends and relations in the films.

94

As stated in the introduction, Justin Brooke, with his fruit farm, dairy, and other interests, was the largest employer in the area between the wars.

June 1982

As a result of boundary changes we learn that the Plumbers Arms will move to Wickhambrook.

It is proposed to straighten out some of the boundaries in Wickhambrook. Denston Plumbers Arms, where at present it is possible to sleep with your feet in Denston and head in Wickhambrook, will be completely in Wickhambrook and Street Farm will be in Denston. All houses on one side of the Bury Road from Manse Row to Sadlers Cottage will be in Denston and all on the other side in Wickhambrook.

August 1982

The Community Council's news page tells us that the Youth Club is again in trouble.

We are sorry to report that the Youth Club, which has been run successfully for the past two years, will possibly not appear this Autumn. One of the facts of life, which although hard to accept but none the less exists, is that the majority suffer for the minority ... A few 'boisterous' (!!) individuals (a gang) have not only put off other youngsters from attending but have made running the evenings' activities extremely difficult, tiring and unrewarding. Those adults who have given up their Tuesday evenings to try to entertain the youth ought to be thanked by the parents. If some parents had offered a little help they might have saved the club, at the same time they might have seen how their children behave 'out of sight out of mind'.

The result of the election to the new Committee of the Community Council is also given. Only five are East Anglian born and of these but two are truly local born. The balance of the 1994 Committee is much the same.

Chairman   – Robert Everitt
Vice-Chairman – Jeff Goodacre
Hon. Secretary – Peter Bayman
Hon. Treasurer – David Turner
Hon. Promoter – Maggie Thearle

The rest of the committee are: Mr Bean (Scene Editor), Mr Crysell, Mr Harrison, Mr Hartshorn, Mr Hicks, Mrs Hines, Mr Long, Mrs Pulford, Mr Lawrence Smith, Mr Les Smith, Mr Thearle and Mr Wyatt.

A plea for help comes from the Recreational Development Committee.

95

Ivan Smith, Graham Steggles, John Smith and a very few others are working hard to build the new pavilion. This pavilion is for the whole village and for all organisations. Can some of you spare a few hours at weekends so that work can be speeded up?

Harold Burton, Chairman of the thriving Horticultural Society and a one time captain of the Wickhambrook Cricket Club, recounts some of his experiences as a young man in the nearby Cambridgeshire Fens, with its strong non-conformist traditions.

A FENLAND PROPHESY

In the more leisurely times of pre-war years there lived in the Fens many smallholders of land. These men were very independent characters and held firm views on most subjects. Many were religiously minded and were prone to using the Bible teachings to back their arguments on most subjects. In fact it could often be said that they had implicit belief in the good book.

One of these smallholders, whose name was Joe, used often to chat to me in the summer evenings and once when it was very hot we were standing at the top of Aldreth Hill, looking across the fenland towards Cambridge, a distance of about ten miles as the crow flies. We had been discussing various matters when suddenly Joe said, 'One day I reckon that will strike and be the end of all of us'. My immediate reaction was 'What will?'. Joe waved his hand towards that great flat fen, where the heat haze shimmered and said bluntly, 'That will'. My look of amazed disbelief did not pass unnoticed for Joe immediately began to support his statement. 'We are getting near to the year two thousand, although I don't suppose I shall be here to see it. World has got to end by then, has it not?'. 'Perhaps', I ventured to say. 'No perhaps about it my boy, you need to read the scriptures; for in the book of Revelations it talks about the great fire coming down from heaven'. I began to see his point and in the end he may be almost right.

Elsewhere it is reported that there is much excitement over Wickhambrook winning three trophies in the Best Kept Village Competition. It won a bowl awarded by the St Edmundsbury District for the best kept village in this area and also the Novices competition. Added to that was the Kenyon Trophy for the Best Kept Village competition for novices in the whole of Suffolk.

October 1982

The final demise of the Harvest Horkey is announced, in the form of a footnote on page 4.

Due to circumstances apparently beyond our control the Harvest Horkey has, regretfully, had to be cancelled for this year.

Derek Pope. Clerk to the Parish Council, asks readers if they are worried by deer.

Wickhambrook Cricket Team in 1885 was a 'temperance' team formed by the Rev John Sharp (seen front left) of the Congregationalists. Only two are in whites, Frank and Percy Woollard, with father Thomas in front centre.

Harvest time at Park Gate Farm, Wickhambrook, 1912.

A 1915 Congregationalist's Sunday School party at Badmondisfield old barn (since burned down). Middle front row with a straw boater is a young Alf Hicks.

On the moat at Badmondisfield Hall in 'Golden Days' around 1910. Left is Miss E Bromley. The Hall was almost destroyed by a fire in February 1995.

The first pension day in Wickhambrook 1908. Pensioners had to be 70 and received 5 shillings. (Some thought it might make them lazy!). The Postmistress was Miss Hannah Brown.

The blacksmiths at Thorns Corner, Wickhambrook, around 1912.

Wickhambrook School 1912. From left: Charlie Wright (a noted Methodist preacher), Miss Farringdon (the photographer's daughter) and Humphrey Eagle.

Ernest Hurrell, Stradishall blacksmith, around 1920. With him his grandson Jim.

Ernie Rowling of the Great Mill delivering bread. His daughter Edna and her husband Ron Penhaligan, and their children, still run the bakery.

The mailman stops for a drink at the Wickhambrook Greyhound around the turn of the century.

Wickhambrook cycling club at Woollards Corner 1908, including members of the Bromley and Woollard families.

The windmill near Thorns Corner 1915 with Mr Bullock the mill owner. Today's shop is to the left of the house.

Busy scene on the Bury Road at Denston Plumbers Arms (left) 1912. The man who moved is believed to be Mr Stephen Kiddy, father of Derek Kiddy of Stradishall.

Paying tribute to Thomas Heigham, Wickhambrook's greatest soldier, at
Wickhambrook Church 1984. Left is Bert Edgeley, the last surviving member
in Wickhambrook of the village's oldest family. Centre, Stan Golding,
right, John Bean.

Justin Brooke's milk roundsmen with their Trojan vans, Clopton, 1929.

Presentation to Mrs Olive Jolly at Wickhambrook School 1990 on her
retirement.

Peter Bayman, Chairman of Wickhambrook Parish Council, and Mrs Bayman (left) greets Princess Anne who arrived on the recreation ground by helicopter, Nov 5, 1979.

Morris dancers at a Wickhambrook Carnival in the eighties.

The successful '93 Football Team, including Jolland brothers Mark, James and Nicholas, and Scott and Derren Williams. Standing left is Steve Jolland, 3rd left, Chris Mortlock and far right Barry Shuter.

Acknowledgments for the use of photographs in this book to: Alf Hicks, 'Bury Free Press', Chris and Peter Mortlock, Frank Claydon, Esme Jolland, Jim Bannister and the Plumbers Arms.

Below: Frank Claydon and passenger 'microlighting' over Wickhambrook.

Arthur and Susannah Pryke, Jack Mortlock's maternal grandparents, kept the Stradishall Hound pub.

This 1859 post box at Boyden End, Wickhambrook, is the only one of its kind in the British Isles. Alf Hicks, wearing his History Society hat, and postman Colin Bird post a letter.

A number of villagers have had damage done to their gardens and fields by herds of deer which seem to be on the increase in this area. Mr Stephen Cham of the British Deer Society is making a survey of deer in Suffolk. He would be interested to have details of any incidents where damage occurs, or of sightings of groups of deer. Information should include date and approximate time, numbers and type (or size) of deer, if known, as well as location. The Clerk would be pleased to pass on any details.

January 1983

During the eighties Wickhambrook's November 5th celebrations grew to be one of the best village events in West Suffolk, under the organisation of Peter Bayman as the chief firework lighter.

The Community Council reports:

The bonfire and fireworks was another successful evening, although we made only a small profit for funds. This may at first seem a contradiction but when you consider we were competing with the big events at Bury St Edmunds, Long Melford, Newmarket and Clare, who have an immediate catchment area, we feel we did quite well against this competition. With a total expenditure of £941.71, to have received £951.17 is an achievement.

The Clerk to the Parish Council gave details of its meeting with the Governor of Highpoint Prison. Main points were:

1. The plans to enlarge Highpoint to bring in Category B inmates and also provide a Detention Centre for young offenders have been dropped.

2. Most inmates are Category C ('do not normally make a determined effort to escape, but not fully suitable for Category D "who can reasonably be trusted to serve out their sentence in open conditions"'). It is planned to increase the number of Category C to 457.

3. There are 60–70 Cat.D inmates at Highpoint now, and the Governor read out an impressive list of tasks completed by these men to help local committees.

At the close of the meeting the Parish Councillors expressed the view that there was no need for anxiety about developments at Highpoint.

Further comment on the Best Kept Village Award, in the form of an anonymous poem. I suspect it was the work of Fred Thearle.

I thought I saw a brand new pub, down in Wickhambrook;
but when I got up to the post and took a further look,
I found it was a sign, a kind of sort of bounty,
To say we were the best kept village in the County.
Now as I gazed up at it, whilst sitting on my bike,
I thought if we were best, what were the others like?

97

But I must not criticise the award that had been won,
For surely we must be Nulli Secondus, and that means second
to none.

May 1983

*Alice Shave, then one of Wickhambrook's oldest inhabitants
recalls the neighbours she had as a girl.*
I live at No. 9 Shop Hill, where I have lived for about 67 years. The
former occupiers, I believe were called Mr and Mrs Crick. The
woman made home-made sweets and sold them from the window of
the house to the children.

There used to be nine houses in this row at one time, but most
were pulled down when they got beyond repair. They were mostly
thatched cottages. The folk who lived there were as follows:

No. 8, Mr & Mrs Wright; No. 7, Mr and Mrs Fred Cook; No. 6,
Mr Will Cook, he was a gardener and also a cobbler and was known
as 'Cobbler Billy'; No. 5, Mr & Mrs Alfred Cook, known as 'Chatty';
No. 4, Mr & Mrs J. Wright, known as 'Blue Dripping'; No. 3, Mr
& Mrs Taylor; No. 2, Mr and Mrs J. Turner, known as 'Jimmy Box',
who were in fact the parents of Mrs Potter of Malting End. No. 1,
was never occupied in my time, but was used by Mr Cook as an out
house to chop wood etc. It was always called 'Tommies'. I daresay
my Dad knew why. He attended the present school the second week
that it was opened in 1878, and that was a very long time ago. Bill
Underwood and his mother came to live at No. 7 in 1927.

In those times it was all so different with high hedges each side of
the roads which were very rough and not very well kept like they are
in this day and age.

*In 'Other Days' Stan Golding quotes from a parish church
vestry meeting document of 24th May, 1813.*
The Tythe of all underwood in the Wickhambrook parish is to the
vicar and taken in kind, except Easty Wood which pays the sum of
ten shillings per annum according to ancient custom. Every Hen or
Duck pays one half penny; Fruit, Pigs, Geese and Honey are taken
in kind, and are other small Tythes and ecclesiastical duties throughout the said Parish belong to the vicar.

There are belonging to the said Parish church one Flagon of Silver,
weighing 36 oz, two Pewter Flaggons and one Pewter Plate, weighing
seven and a half pounds; one Challice with cover of silver, weighing
13 oz.

The six signatories to these extracts from a document of 1813 were
described as Principal Inhabitants of the Parish.

Nathaniel Bradley	Radclyffe Smoothley
Thomas Hines	James Last
Radley Hockly	George Pryke

July 1983

The Community Council reports on its planning for this year's annual Carnival.

At our May meeting we had discussion planning the Children's Sports and the Carnival Queen and Princesses competition, both events having been and gone.

We were a little disappointed that there were not more children joining in the sports, which we are sure were enjoyed by those who were there. As usual a good attendance of mums, dads and children who witnessed the choosing of the Queen, Rosalyn Carpenter and the two Princesses, Heidi Dalton and Margaret Fairburn. Our thanks to all those who helped to make these two events so successful.

September 1983

'THE SHOW'S GOING DOWN HILL'

Both Alf Hicks, writing as secretary of the Horticultural Society, and Peter Bayman, as Community Council Secretary, reported that adverse comments had been made about the Carnival Day. Alf:

Some comments were: 'The Show's going down hill'. 'No band'. 'No Fair'. 'No Bar'. 'Nothing for the children, such as sports, magicians or Punch & Judy'. Others said it lacked atmosphere.

Peter Bayman:

The Carnival, which financially was a great success, left us with several thoughts for next year. Suffice to say we are aware that the carnival atmosphere has gone or is certainly not what it used to be and we will have discussions in the Autumn to try to rectify some of our shortcomings.

At the Autumn meeting, the Editor, supported by others, suggested that we must bring back music, either via the fair or from a band, and also bring back a stewarded licenced bar.

The 'Brigadier' (in reality none other than Alf Hicks) gives his usual report on the activities of the local Company of the Boys Brigade, the 8th Mid Suffolk.

This Centenary year of The Boys Brigade, founded by Sir Alexander Smith in Glasgow in 1883, is proving to be an active and exciting one. The Eastern District had a great day on the Suffolk Show Ground at Ipswich on June 25th when over 8000 people including Brigade officers, boys, parents and friends witnessed the Show Fanfare.

Boys and officers of the 8th Mid Suffolk Company (*the local company*) took part in events in the Arena. Demonstrations, competitions, history and games all caused interest to young and old alike on a day that will long be remembered. On the Sunday there was an open air service Interdenominational . . .

Our Company's Camp once again has been thoroughly enjoyed, this year at Cleethorpes. Several of us have been going for 30 years.

Peter Place of Bury at 73 has been coping since he was a boy of 13, when the cost was 10 shillings per boy!

November 1983

The Clerk to the Parish Council makes a plea for caution in straw burning.
At their September meeting the Parish Council discussed the straw burning problem. It was pointed out that some farmers had kept to the NFU Code and ought to be thanked for their consideration. There were others, however, whose burning activities had caused a great deal of damage, distress and disgust. Plans are being made by the Parish Council which it is hoped will ensure that we do not suffer next year as we have this.

Several tributes are paid to Mrs Ivy Hicks, wife of Alf, who died suddenly and unexpectedly.

In his 'Other Days' column Stanley Golding gives us some of the results of his researches into the origins of the Almshouses next to Wickhambrook Parish Church.
Anthony Sparrow, of Depden, in the 11th year of the reign of King James the First, had a house built 'neare to ye church, divided into sixe severall dwelling rooms for housing ye aged poore.'

In 1615 he charged Stansfield Mill a yearly payment of £8 for the relief of the poor, £3 of which was to be divided among inmates of the almshouse in Wickhambrook. 'To ye poore of Depden, fourty shillings and four pence; to Denstoun and Stansfield thirteen shillings and four pence each; to Chedburgh and Haukedon each tenne shillings.'

In his will, proved in 1617, Anthony bequeathed a yearly payment of £3 to be divided between 'maydens of fourty years and upwards; or, if none, to wydoes having neither childe nor childer; or to some lone man in ye parish of threescore yeres and upwards. And my will and meaning is that this payment shall be made through church-wardens.'

Anthony died in 1617 and is buried in the chancel of All Saints' church.

A wall tablet is inscribed: These Almshouses were restored in 1897 by Friends of the Poor of Wickhambrook, part of the cost being defrayed by relatives, in memory of Nathaniel Warner Bromley, Esquire, of Badmondesfield Hall.

January 1984

Not for the first time, I had to apologise to readers for the fact that 'The Scene' was again late.
. . . When the Community Council decided to change our publishing dates so that the first issue of 'The Scene' in each year started with January–February, instead of there being a December–January

100

issue as previously, the problems created by producing the new issue over the Christmas period were not fully appreciated. But the suggestion came too late and rather assumed that your editor could wave his magic wand and get all contributions in within two days and that our typist, Margaret Elers, could drop everything else (including her children?) a week before Christmas to do the rough typing and then the typing of the stencils from my lay-out in another day. The next stage is to hand these stencils over to our worthy printers, Fred Thearle and Tom Ming. Then, the same two gentlemen, aided and abetted by Maggie Thearle, have to collate the pages together (slip one in upside down just to check that you read it) and also put them inside the advertising covers. So you see, there is quite a lot in producing 'The Scene'.

May 1984

Alf Hicks gives details from a letter he has received from Mrs Hilda Dean, a daughter of Dr Robert Wilkin, Wickhambrook's long serving GP at the end of the last century and the early part of this.

Dr Stutters (*whose diaries were found in the attic of Brooke Cottage and extracts from which appeared in October 1969 and November 1984*) proceeded her grandfather (Dr W. L. Wilkin) as the village Doctor, who lived in Wash Lane. When her father qualified he moved to Beechwood (*still in Wickhambrook*) and had an extension built, two bathrooms and two lavatories. Dr R. H. Wilkin had the first car locally and David Foster drove it. Dr J. D. Batt became his assistant and lived first of all at Denston before moving to the Old White Horse (*formerly a pub*) opposite the church, where his son, the present Dr B. J. Batt, is still living.

She remembers the three banks in the village: Hill House, formerly the Crown Inn; the Reading Room at Thorns; and the White Horse – only Lloyds kept on after 1940. She opened her first account at the Lloyds branch with the late Clement Fuller. She also well remembers the brick kiln at Coltsfoot Green and played there with her brothers and sisters as a girl.

Her sister Joyce lived at Genesis Green at the time the Dornier Flying Pencil bomber came down behind the Gesyns Farm on a spot where Lidgate, Ousden and Wickhambrook meet. Mr Firth, a gamekeeper, came out of a wood with a pitch fork and the crew of five surrendered! (*It was returning from the Luftwaffe raid on Coventry.*)

As a little girl she was much intrigued when visiting Mrs Hannah Brown, the post mistress, that there was a three tier outside toilet: Dad, Mum and baby.

E. S. (Stan) Golding gives us the results of his latest researches at the Bury St Edmunds Records Office.

All Saints, Wickhambrook.

Sir George Somerset, born at Badmondesfield Hall, was buried in an altar tomb within the Sanctuary, on the left side of the East window. Octobris 16, 1590.

Sir George was the 3rd son of Charles Somerset, Earl of Worcester, who, in 1524, gave the manor of Badmondesfield and other manors within the parish of Wickhambrook to his wife Eleanor, her children and heirs. The estate had been bought from Richard Grey, Earl of Kent. John de Hastings, the elder, was Lord of the Manor in 1311.

The altar tomb, stone altar and other monuments were either desecrated or destroyed by the Puritans during the Civil War, including tablets upon which were inscribed The Lord's Prayer, Beliefs and the Ten Commandments.

Home Office Papers, 1868.

. Complaints against Ensign Levell of the Eastern Battalion of the East Suffolk Militia that he had lately hired an alehouse in Ipswich, and by taking up so low and contemptible a profession has brought discredit upon the corps in which he serves as an officer, that they (his fellows) will no longer serve with him; nor, indeed, would his lordship (Lord Orwell) in a service so much debased by being united to the lowest of all trades, exercised by the dregs of the people.

July 1984

As editor, I applaud the fact that several young people have joined the Community Council Committee. Unfortunately, only two lasted the pace.

No doubt partly as a result of our plea for support in both the last issue of 'The Scene' and also the last 'What's On', it was great to see 50 people in attendance at our Annual General Meeting last month. What is more, many of us thought it was very gratifying to see an age spread of between 14 and 74 – with all ports of call in between!

Now, although I appreciate that some of the youngsters came along 'for a laugh' (Yes, we were *all* young once), it is good news to report that some of them have now joined the Community Council Committee and we trust that they will continue to put forward some of the ideas they expressed at the AGM, coupled with some positive help.

Harold Burton again reminisces about his boyhood days in the Fens.

A DAY FISHING 1926

My friend Reggie and I lived in a Fenland village and although there were a number of small canals within a mile or so of our homes, the river, the old west course of the Great Ouse, was almost three miles away. I was ten and he was a little older. Reggie always thought that it was better to go the extra distance as the fish in the river would give us more sport and that the chance of catching a 'whopper' would

102

be greater. He was probably right but that was not all the story, for we had no bicycles and therefore had to walk all the way, unless a kindly farmer allowed us to ride in his tumbril cart, which although not so hard on the legs was no speedier way of travel. Apart from the extra distance it meant that fishing time was much less than if we stopped at one of the canals nearer home. Nevertheless, we almost invariably went to the river. This took about one and a half hours journey time. This was a large slice of the time allowed us by our parents for the treat.

We were given thick cheese sandwiches and a bottle of drinking water, left home about nine in the morning and told to be home for tea not later than five o'clock. This was in the school summer holidays and a change from routine. I should add that we had no watch and had to guess the time by the sun. We became rather good at that as we would have been prevented from going again had we gone against parents orders.

Our tackle was quite primitive by today's standards. My grandfather grew osiers, as he was in the basket making business, so he provided the rods; willow ones about eight feet long with a three-quarter inch butt. These he sold to the lads of the village at three-halfpence each; to us they were free. We each had a brown water cord line, price twopence; three halfpenny hooks to gut, which we tied on to the line, for spares; four eel hooks which cost a penny and a float made out of a bottle cork through which we had passed a trimmed turkey quill. This cost nothing.

We had some dry crusts, which we soaked, for catching rudd, roach and bream and some tiger worms for perch, and as alternative bait for other fish if they appeared not to be taking the bread. The worms we dug from the edge of a muck-hill in Hoghill Drover on our way to the river.

Our catch on a good day after six hours, perhaps one roach of half a pound and three or four of two ounces each, a four ounce rudd and a perch of six ounces, two or three bleak of no sufficient weight and usually a gudgeon. The larger fish were taken home in triumph, cleaned and cooked for breakfast the next day. We pretended we liked them, but my recollections are that they had to be smothered with vinegar to camouflage the muddy flavour and that they were full of small bones and in no way comparable to a herring which could be bought for a penny at that time. The fishing in the river was however great fun and I am sure the walking did us no harm.

September 1984
The editor reports on what appears to be some small success in the campaign to preserve our remaining hedgerows.

Mr Lee of Justin Brooke informs me that they will shortly be undertaking considerable work on hedgerow management. I am assured that this will not entail the removal of any more hedges, but in some areas where hedges have not been touched for many years it will mean that they will need to be coppiced down to ground level. Now before any of you (with whom it is known I have considerable sympathy, even empathy) phone me or write about what at first may appear to be elimination of more hedges, please read the article (elsewhere in the issue) on 'Hedgerow Management' by Melinda Appleby, the Farm Conservation Advisory Officer for Suffolk County Council. This will explain fully what is going on and why.

Stan Golding supplies an extract from the Edgeley Family Tree. Herbert is the sole surviving direct descendant of Henry Edgeley (1625–1701) to have been born and still living in the parish. *(He died since this was written).* Each and every one of his seven ancestors were born, lived and died in the village – a truly remarkable and unbroken link with the past 360 years. There are of course, countless others who can claim a like descent, but not living in Wickhambrook. Bernard Edgley of Depden is one who can.

All the children of James Edgeley (1851) were born in the old workhouse, which had been purchased by his father.

Henry c1625–1701	= Elizabeth – 1701 Henry's will at Bury
Henry	= Elizabeth Parmand Bap. Lt. Thurlow, 1656 Married at Gr. Bradley
Henry 1695–1756	= Mary Young (i) Mary (ii) 15 children born of two marriages.
John 1775–1846	= Mary (Dolly) Pearson (i) – 1805 Jemima Pearson (ii) 1783–1855
James 1813–1890	= Ann Taylor
James 1851–1909	= Helen Dutton 1851–1935
Herbert 1876–1957	= J.P. (i) Lucy Jane (ii) Buried 1958, (79).
Herbert 1906–	

*Excerpts from the day books and papers of Dr W. G. Stutter,
Medical Attendant to Wickhambrook and surrounding villages in
early Victorian times, had already been published in 'The Scene'
in October 1969. The new owners of Brook Cottage, Cloak
Lane, David and Claire Tomsett, where Dr Stutter had lived,
loaned them to Jack Mortlock to prepare further extracts.*

Names of patients, their addresses or location, their occupation, their
treatment as well as other information were recorded. Patients were
spread over a very wide area. Moulton and Ashley in the north,
Hundon and Poslingford in the south, Rede and Whepstead in the
east, over to Withersfield and Kirtling in the west and all places in
between. Family names still well known in the area occur frequently:
Metcalf, Wiseman, Edgeley, Mortlock, Pryke, Pask and others.

Dr Stutter's writing (with a quill pen of course) was like so many
doctors, almost illegible. Some of it was so bad that I suspect he may
have made the books up whilst riding his horse. One entry read:
'Rising during night – attend patient at Ashley – return in morning,
charge 3/6d' (17½p). As far as I can ascertain a man in full employment at that time could earn 8/- a week (40p), so perhaps it wasn't
such a bad night's work.

It took me a little while to fathom out the word 'pills'. The doctor
wrote it always fading the second 'l' into an 'e'. For a time I thought
there seemed to be quite a lot of haemorrhoids around in the district.
Another entry that appeared very often, was fitting of a truss – even
to young boys of nine and ten years. I suppose with youngsters doing
very heavy work it wasn't so unusual. The price seemed to range
between 5/- and £1.

Here are some odd jottings from these papers.

Mr Cook, Wickham Street (Drover). Extract piece of steel from
his eye. Feb 1842.

Mr J. Smith, 1843. Extracting stone from son's ear 2/6.

A little servant girl, treatment. Mr Eagle of Cowlinge promised to
pay.

Mr Cheesebait of Barrow had treatment 1843. He was a ratcatcher.

Maria Bonnett examined for rape – committed Aug. 9th 1857.

Robert Rutter a soldier 43 Regt of Londonderry had treatment
1842.

James Hines, a butcher. Mr Perry, a shoemaker. Will Brown, a
schoolmaster. Carter, a watchmaker. Woollard, a miller. Mr Chap-
man, a tinker. Gilby, a saddler. Will Turner, a colt breaker. All had
treatment.

It was noticeable in these papers that Dr Stutter had most of the
local gentry among his patients. The residents of Denston Hall,
Dalham Hall, Stradishall Place, Branches Park, etc. The Rev. Lloyd
was the parson at Cowlinge at the time and lived at Branches Park.

He had at least a dozen servants who were patients of the doctor's: the butler, footman, coachman, housekeeper, maids, gardeners, etc. Those were the days, of course, when parsons usually came from wealthy families; the brightest son into the army, the less bright became the parson. When making entries into his daybook the gentry had esquire after their names. Their children were referred to as Master John, Miss Penelope, for example. In ordinary families they were just recorded as boys and girls.

A Captain Collins of New House, Wickhambrook was a regular patient over several years – dressings to his legs. I wonder was it gout or could he have been wounded at Waterloo? There was no record of him ever paying his bills, perhaps the Army took care of that.

The doctor often put little notes by a person's name. Typical were:

Mr Smith next Church Stradishall; Mrs Simpson the Fox, Ousden; Mr Brown one arm Cowlinge; Mr Gudgeon one eye near Chapel Hargrave; Joe Stiff Cock Hundon. This last entry I had to read two or three times to make sure it was the man's address and not his physical condition.

From the Doctor's papers it seems that all the villages seemed to have a policeman, including one at Depden Green. Stradishall was able to boast of a Superintendent of Police. His name was Death. There wasn't any messing about with probation or suspended sentences at that time. Stealing a loaf of bread or knocking the odd pheasant off was at least a seven year trip to Van Dieman's Land or Botany Bay. Anything more serious could mean hanging or transportation for life. And they call them the 'good old days.'

January 1985

John Long retired from farming at Peacocks farm and moved to the nearby village of Little Thurlow. He wrote to thank everybody for the presentation made to him and his wife Helen in the Memorial Hall which had been contributed to by many local organisations.

I came to Wickhambrook thirty years ago, very broke but with plenty of energy both to work the farm and do a certain amount of Community work. The main challenge came in 1966 when the Social Centre finances were at rock bottom and something had to be done. We formed the Community Council and during the last eighteen years we have achieved a tremendous amount. This has only been done through marvellous team work and a wonderful team of which for many years, I was proud to be their leader.

There were many ups and downs, a few mistakes, but no failures because we do not accept failure. It is always a challenge to go on and eventually get it right. It has proved this by the fact we now have one of the best Social Centres in the Rural Areas of East Anglia.

106

The activities that are now carried out in the Centre makes it difficult for the booking manager to fit any more in. This does not mean we should stand still, there are many more projects which can yet be considered and when funds become available I am sure they will.

I sincerely hope that this community spirit which now exists will bring out more people to become involved on committees. Success is a great reward and no one is ever really too busy to give a helping hand.

Typical of the other projects that John Long referred to was the pavilion, now rising from its foundations. Perry Morley, secretary of the Recreational and Development Fund, writes of the huge commitment made by a few.

I am sure that the many who have contributed will in no way deny the effort of those I mention. Graham Steggles, Ivan Smith and John Smith have been burdened with the foundation and brickwork. Although the work is complete their enthusiasm and commitment remain. Steve Jolland with the help of his sons has undertaken the roof fabrication. A huge task which is now almost finished. Now the committee has learnt that Bob Cross will provide the skills for the electrical installation. The building will be a monument to their labours.

Unless we find a plasterer in the next few months, we will, unfortunately, have to approach sub-contractors from outside the village.

March 1985

Jack Mortlock stated that his extracts from the books and papers of Dr G. Stutter had been well received, with reporters from the 'East Anglian Daily Times' and the 'Bury Free Press' calling to talk to him. He gave us some further comments of his own on the methods of treatment at the time – comments that were coloured by his own sense of humour. He did reveal, however, that in the great Asian Cholera epidemic of 1848, Ipswich, Bury and Norwich got off quite lightly compared to some towns and cities and in the local rural area Dr Stutter reported only two cases: Matilda Humble, aged 11, and Maria Cousins, aged 16. Both were put in Risbridge Union isolation and after about three months treatment happily recovered.

In addition to all his regular reports, Alf Hicks had something to say on the preservation of local historical barns, which had previously been raised by the Parish Council Clerk.

I remember two very big thatched barns at Attleton Green. The late Mr Tom Claydon and his young wife Edith (still living and always reminds me of the Queen Mother) had not been there long when there was a big fire destroying them both and the house also caught fire (*see entry for June 1969*).

Mr Will King (*lay preacher at the United Reform Church*) of course owns one of the finest old barns in the village. There used to be one at Street Farm where Mr and Mrs E. Honeyball now live and can be seen on old photographs. Other barns are at Peacocks Farm, Farley Green, and Park Gate (now falling down!). There were at one time barns all over the place, but they are fast disappearing. The thatched barns were always in danger, sparks from steam engines driving threshing tackles spelled doom to quite a number.

I remember when the house now known as Willow Cottage at the entrance to Coltsfoot Close was thatched. Although not a barn, it was almost as big! Two of us boys sat on the top of the thatch, armed with long sticks to beat out any flying burning straw blowing in the wind that might settle. We succeeded and received 5/- reward!

P.S. I think we ought to form a Historical Society in our village to really probe into the past.

May 1985

The death is reported of Mr William (Will) King. In addition to his work for Wickhambrook United Reformed Church, and its regular reporter to 'The Scene', he was also Chairman of the Horticultural Society. He was succeeded in this latter post by Mr Robert (Bobby) Cook.

The guest at a recent Horticultural Society social evening had been local shepherd Richard Seabrook of TV fame at that time. He too was to die (of cancer) within four years.

September 1985

CREATING A COLONY OF PROSPERITY

Alf Hicks pays his respects to the memory of Mrs R. E. Brooke, widow of Justin Brooke, who had died the previous month at her Clopton Hall home.

She was a lady held in high respect and affection, who came with her husband, the late Mr Justin Brooke, to our village over 50 years ago. What a great impact they made on Wickhambrook.

Creating a colony of prosperity, in the time of great depression, they helped to end class distinction and I well remember Mr Brooke saying 'I look forward to the time when all my men will own motor cars'. Mrs Brooke to the end was concerned about people and the Clopton colony was her family. Young married couples could go confidently to them for advice.

Inspired by them both we were able to do things that we thought were impossible.

As one of those who was with them from the start until war came, I shall always be grateful to the memory of Mrs Brooke, and of course, to that dynamo of vision and action, Justin Brooke.

Considerable correspondence, including from the Rural Dean, has been generated by Stanley Golding's letter in the previous issue alleging that the Vicar, Bill Davies, had refused to baptise some babies. As editor I attempted to suggest what the Vicar's motives really were.

It would appear from the airing of views that the Vicar has never point blank refused to baptise a child, even if he may have appeared to. His strong insistence that parents and godparents should take baptism seriously and understand what it entails, and that it is not just another festival that has lost its meaning, has obviously upset some parents.

January 1986

Somebody calling himself 'Clay Jurd' sends a copy of some verse he had sent to friends in Dorset who had enquired about the nature of our soil.

You asked what sort of soil we have,
and I much regret to say,
that, in our part of Suffolk
it is clay, and clay and CLAY!

Heavy, mutinous, glutinous stuff
with a will all of its own.
And every forkful that you dig
weighs round about a stone.

You can dig it, prod or rake it,
or push and pull – or yank it.
It still sticks to every tool you use
like treacle to a blanket.

It'll glue yer wellies to the ground,
(Which ain't a pretty sight)
In emergencies we use it here
instead of Araldite.

Don't ask me what the pee aitch is,
I really wouldn't know.
All that I can tell you is –
it don't half make things grow.

Well – that is if you're fit and strong
and you don't mind sweat and toil.
Which only goes to show that –
The answer's 'in the soil.'

March 1986

A number of reports appeared in the 'East Anglian' and 'Bury Free Press' on the objections expressed by many local people

109

*on the development going on in the Nunnery Green/Boyden Close
area of Wickhambrook. One St Edmundsbury Borough
Council Official displayed his ignorance of the nature of the
problem when he said:*
'Strictly speaking development on this scale in any Other Village is
contrary to policy. However, Nunnery Green is a large village with
a good range of facilities and public transport links.'
*In reality Nunnery Green is just one of the eleven greens that
make up Wickhambrook and before development was hardly the
size of a hamlet. Its 'public transport links' were and are nil.*
*I tried to sum up the objections of the local people to this excess
development in 'The Scene' editorial page.*
As the Clerk (Derek Pope) to our Parish Council says, the confusion
is 'over the way the Borough altered its planning application for
development at the end of Nunnery Green.' Those of us who supported Mr Cliff Moore in his petition did so in the main because this
whole development, and not just the twelve dwellings for older folk
(originally it was going to be 20), was NOT what we expected it to
be from the original outline plans that we were shown some 12 years
ago. It has now been turned into the erection of a mini 'Newtown'
right in the middle of a rural village.

In the 1976 Suffolk Structural Plan, Wickhambrook is listed as a
Category C village. This means that the only building development
allowed is 'infilling', i.e. between existing buildings. It would appear
that Mr Johnson and his crew in the St Edmundsbury Planning
Committee and associated Department, have thrown our Category
C listing out of the window.

Where the blame cannot be laid, as some people erroneously think,
is at the door of our Parish Council. Their powers are limited on this
matter and they can only recommend and pass on our views, which
they have done.

May 1986

*John Long, as Wickhambrook's District Councillor at
St Edmundsbury Borough Council, made his reply to the previous
issue's airing of the Nunnery Green 'Newtown'.*
I have had two or three meetings with Mr Johnson – the Planning
Officer and Mr Albon the Chief Technical Officer of the Borough
Council – to find ways of preserving an open space in this part of
Nunnery Green. Also of persuading the Council to build a block of
sheltered accommodation for this Ward. It was found that the most
economical block would have been 25–26 units with warden control.
This was eventually ruled out because of both enormous expense and
that this number was far in excess of what was required. Recently,
however, the Housing Association – a private concern, hence the
changes of planning application – came forward with the proposition

to purchase the site to erect 12 purpose built Old People's Units. The number of course would not take up the whole of the 2 acre site.

On invitation I attended the Planning Committee Meeting when this was discussed and what should happen to the remainder of the site. The Chairman gave me the opportunity to give my views, which I expressed in the strongest terms that having fought for so long for Old Peoples accommodation I fully supported the Housing Association's plan but in no way would I support the plan to sell off the remainder for private development. I stated that this area should be left as an open space for a safe children's play area and the only building to be considered in the future would be an extension of the Old People's units. This was accepted by the committee for the present time. It will be up to future DCs, myself, if elected, to carry on the demand for no more development.

Alf Hicks had something new to report in this issue: the formation of Wickhambrook Local History Society. Mrs Brenda Fairhall was appointed Secretary; Mrs Dianne Everitt, Treasurer; and Alf Hicks, Chairman. Committee members were Miss Ruth Smart, Mrs Dorothy Anderson, Mr E. Garner and Mr R. Medcalf.

Member very much appreciated a visit from Mr H. V. Haygreen with his slides showing scenes of over 50 years ago. These included the three mills – all now disappeared, the old shop near the school run by Mr & Mrs Hinds before the First World War, where you could buy a farthing's worth of sweets. He also showed pictures of threshing tackles, old tractors, steam rollers rolling in the granite chippings on the roads. Newcomers to the village who were present at the meeting were very interested.

July 1986

According to the Clerk to the Parish Council, Derek Pope, the two main items under discussion were the development of the Recreational Ground, and tackling the growing problem of burglary and theft. (It was about this time that the village shop and post office was burgled twice in three weeks. In both cases thieves knocked a hole in the wall and drove off with the post office safe.)

Before the 'Six Acres' of land (behind the present Recreation Ground) can be developed for recreational purposes it will be necessary for this land to be properly drained to a standard suitable for playing fields ...

... At the recent Police Forum we were given helpful advice on crime prevention. One very important thing is to mark valuable items with your postcode and initials. Recently stolen property of consider-

111

able value which was recovered in a south coast town was returned to its Suffolk owner, because he had taken the trouble to postcode his property.

Do you or your children own bikes? Have them properly marked (the Police will do this at no cost to you). Then if they are stolen, you stand a better chance of getting them back.

Wearing a different hat, as a staunch member of the United Reformed Church and occasional lay preacher, Derek Pope also informs us that the church building at Meeting Green has just been listed as of Special Architectural and Historic Interest.

The Chapel was built in 1743 by the local congregation of Independents. It is described as being 'in red brick, with an admixture of blue bricks, laid in Flemish bond.' The two long windows at the rear are original, 'with semi-circular heads and diamond-leaded panes; divided into three by heavy glazing bars, and with small opening casement with pintle hinges in the central division.'

The two main doorways are also original 'with plain surrounds, segmented arches and fine doors, each with eight raised and fielded panels.' The inspectors were impressed by the original iron foot scrapers and the 'ornate bracketed lamp-holder with decorative finial on top,' and also by the roof – 'an ingenious structure of cast iron and timber with cast iron ties and timber queen struts and purlins.'

In his 'Other Days' column, Stan Golding reminds us of the other face of 'Merry England' four centuries ago.

THE BURY MARTYRS

In the reign of Queen Mary seventeen protestants suffered death (mainly by burning at the stake) at Bury St Edmunds. Their names are inscribed on a monument at the end of the avenue in St Mary's churchyard.

Philip Humfrey, burned in 1553.
John Abbes, a youth of Stoke by Nayland, burned in 1555.
Adam Foster, husbandman, Mendlesham.
John Cooke, Sawyer, Stoke by Nayland.
Alexander Lane, wheelwright, Stoke by Nayland, burned 1555.
Roger Clarke, Mendlesham.
John and Henry David, brothers.
James Ashley, bachelor.
Thomas Parret, Martin Hunt, John Norse.
Thomas Spurdance, a servant of the Queen, burned in 1557.
Roger Bernard, burned in 1557, a labourer.
John Dale, weaver, of Hadleigh, died in gaol, 1558.
Robert Miles, shearman.

September 1986

Perhaps inspired by Stan Golding's account of the Bury Martyrs, Jack Mortlock, his verbal sparring partner in The Cloak, had submitted an article headed: 'A Nasty Piece of Work'

William Dowsing, a man born and bred in the rather attractive village of Laxfield near Framlingham, became the Arch Vandal of Suffolk during the Cromwell Commonwealth period.

His job was to rid the churches of religious pictures including stained glass and all other superstitious objects. He carried out this work with great enthusiasm and thoroughness. Its recorded that he dealt with 150 churches in 50 days. A brief report was rendered to his superiors after each assignment. For our village it may have read thus:-

Wickhambrook All Saints 23 Nov 1648

Removed or destroyed 17 statues, escutcheons, (name plates on coffins, shields etc.) and paintings. All stained glass knocked out from the inside.

Sundry superstitious objects, emblems and signs of Popery removed.

We then proceeded to Denardiston (Denston).

Our vicar at that time the Rev. Thomas Gray may have witnessed this desecration and vandalism with horror, but was quite powerless to prevent it. He was replaced in the following year by Rev. John Cooper who was appointed by the Puritan Commissioners.

Many people thought that this man Dowsing would be severely punished after the death of Cromwell and the restoration of Charles II in 1660.

He in fact returned to his home village, kept a 'low profile' and went unpunished for the rest of his life.

Rain reduced the attendance considerably at this year's Carnival. However, the Editor notes that the return of the bar, after an absence of four years helped to alleviate the situation.

Our nearly finished pavilion was the venue for the bar: packed with people taking a breather from the rain, some of them on soft drinks only, others not so, but nobody causing a nuisance. Let us be honest, without that focal point where people could gather together, converse and joke about the atrocious weather, the recreation ground would have been deserted by 4.00 p.m.

January 1987

The Editor muses over the festive season good will and good humour.

... It is early New Year's Eve as I write this – and I may not be able to see the typewriter keys tomorrow. You may have your moans at times, but think how lucky you are to live in Wickhambrook. I visited a few local establishments over the holiday period and never heard a word raised in anger (not even when someone drank my beer). Elsewhere you would have a good chance of being mugged, murdered, raped or assaulted. Could it just be that we have the right 'mix' of people here – in all senses of the word?

Jo Jurd, in his 'Village Verse' is also given to musing, with his memories of yesteryear.

When only the wealthy had 'wireless',
And that new-fangled electric lighting;
You would probably think our childhood days
Were tedious, and unexciting.
For whatever did we find to do
Before computers and television;
Or stereos, videos, discos, pop,
Space games – and nuclear fission?

Well, we found joy in simpler things,
(We weren't sophisticated!)
Like family readings from a book –
Which today seems very dated.
And artless games, like Snakes and Ladders,
Ludo and Meccano;
Or 'Just a Song at Twylight'
Sung around the old piano.

And what a great event it was –
The memory still abides –
When at the Village Hall they showed
Those Magic Lantern slides!
Yes, we had simple homespun fun –
You can see we weren't too clever –
Yet happily at Wickhambrook,
Those days aren't gone for ever!

For at the Horticultural Supper
There was food, and fun, and games;
And Ron and Horace entertained us
With their 'Magic Lantern' frames!
And recapturing those dear dead days,
(Though he didn't bring Meccano!)
Was Sidney, singing oldtime songs,
Whilst Vincent played piano!

March 1987

It is announced that John Long, District Councillor for the Wickhambrook Ward, has been appointed Mayor elect for St Edmundsbury (Bury St Edmunds and surrounding parishes) – a new feather in Wickhambrook's hat.

Congratulations to John Long and his wife Helen, who will be the Mayoress, from all on the Wickhambrook Community Council! He has been our representative on the St Edmundsbury Council for the last nine years and a Parish Councillor for over 12 years. John was also one of the founder members of the Wickhambrook Community Council and was Chairman of the Committee for at least 12 years until he voluntarily stood down to let some younger blood get into action. He is still a member of the Committee and perhaps he will turn up at our next meeting wearing the Mayor's chain of office!

'The Scene' had acquired two new writers, who were both very different from the long established contributors and also from each other. One was 'Barfly', alias Bernard Young, an assistant Governor at Highpoint Prison; the other was 'Messenger', alias Colin Bird, the local Postman. The Editor's problem was to get the former to comment on the local world outside of the esoteric confines of the Plumbers Arms, and to get the latter to bring his anecdotal observations on the world at large into the local patch of Wickhambrook and West Suffolk.

A typical Barfly contribution appeared in this issue and is published here with 'identification notes' in parenthesis for those who do not frequent the Plumbers Arms.

Christmas and the New Year have now passed and the little world in which we live still flourishes. The snow and cold have been difficult but we have not detracted from the real issues. Our man from the F.O. *(Roger Dennis, who once worked for the Foreign Office)* came in and having grasped a pint made a request in general but to the Patriarch *(the landlord, whose greying hair is shoulder length)* in particular for some old newspapers. Apparently he has acquired a new puppy dog whose education is proving hazardous. I find it hard to believe that he is teaching the animal to read.

The balls on the pool table are clacking away and Our Man from Galicia *(Manuel, a local resident Spanish psychiatrist)* is engaged in almost mortal combat with Steve the Prudent *(Steve Williams, who works for Prudential Assurance)*. 'Filth!' Steve cries as he is left with an awkward shot. But he manages to get out of the fix by a crafty rebound off the cushion and the balls gradually disappear until only the white and black remain.

The Super Vacuum Cleaner Salesman and Manufacturer *(Mick Prigg, a local engineer who had designed his Terravac powerful cleaner)* is trying to warm himself by the fire and berating the Patriarch over his parsimony in the provision of wood to burn, even though he has burnt half the timber which was supposed to hold up my house which Compo *(Eric Bowers, a freelance builder who dresses 'Compo' style)* has had to rip out and replace with building blocks to stop it from falling down.

Monsieur Haricot *(Bean)* arrived the other night having had difficulty in getting back here. Little wonder as the prairies of East Anglia have encouraged the snow to drift onto the roads. Although we are better blessed than other areas, so many hedges have been grubbed out to the detriment of the fauna and to the increment of the European Grain Mountain, that we must be grateful to the local farmers for their help in digging us out and keeping us from being cut off.

Nevertheless, the year could be exciting; threats of a General Election, plus the donation of a year's subscription to *Private Eye* for the Patriarch's customers by the Producer *(Richard Beighton, a local resident TV producer)*.

From the start 'Messenger' was consistent in showing his concern for the suffering that is sometimes inflicted upon animals.
... I was shocked and appalled to hear from a worker at the chicken processing plant in Bury, that many of the birds were being delivered dead on arrival – literally frozen to death in their cramped and overcrowded cages. I have felt sick to the stomach, when in the past I have witnessed these lorries speeding through the village in the early hours, trailing down and feathers in their wake and piled high with crate upon crate packed with wretched, and no doubt, terrified birds. But how much worse than even this, when no provision is made for these unfortunate creatures during the ravages of the January weather when temperatures plummeted to −10C.

I find it sad when we can all rally round so spectacularly in defence of our own kind in times of natural disaster and crisis, and yet barely give a thought for other species on whom we pile indignity and cruelty so frequently.

July 1987

The elections for the Parish Council had been held, resulting in three long serving councillors losing their seats. They were, surprisingly, John Long, Alf Hicks and the Rev. Bill Davies. Perhaps it was down to 'new' voters as only two (Vic Harrod and Jeff Claydon) were born in the village and only another two of the seven elected had lived here for more than twenty years. The results were:

Colin Bird 254, Peter Bayman (Chairman) 246, Mrs Brenda Fairhall 241, Mrs Barbara Merritt 224, Jeff Claydon 205, Robert Everitt 201, Vic Harrod 195. Not elected: John Long 181, Alf Hicks 178, Mick Prigg 167, Mrs Lesley Williams 164, Ron Corbyn 131, Kerry Merritt 109, Rev. Bill Davies 72.

September 1987

Throughout this year we were very preoccupied with the weather, but at least it stayed fine for the Carnival day. The Editor observes:
As I write this, the edge of my lawn has just appeared from under the receding floodwater that engulfed the crossroads at Attleton Green. The last vestiges of the eight-year-old cow muck that I was

inveigled to buy from Billy Wright has disappeared from the rose beds. Washed away by the floods, it is probably in the North Sea by now: if not giving nourishment to some Dutchman's garden in the Hook of Holland.

The recent flood was indicative of the abysmal summer we have had this year in the East of the Country. However, we should at least be thankful that the Carnival and Flower Show day was blessed by unusual fine weather, which played its part in drawing a crowd of over a thousand (that includes those who come through the hedges); the best for several years. If you read the balance sheet figures for the day in our centrespread you will see that apart from providing a good day for all visitors, which I contend is the *main* objective, we also made a profit of £420, which the Community Council splits in a 60:40 ratio with the Horticultural Society.

Stan Golding was to write his last 'Other Days' column, as provocative as ever. It seemed he knew his time was coming, for he was to die in December in his 91st year.

In Memoriam

Thomas Heigham, of 'Gyffords', a distinguished Elizabethan soldier, patriot and devout Christian, died on the 15th day of August, 1631, and buried in an altar tomb in the sanctuary of All Saints' church.

'Who would true valour see, let him come hither.'

Old Man's Tale

All, all are gone, the old familiar faces – Lamb.

Living in a world with which he is no longer familiar, what can an old man do but think upon times past, the days that are no more.

Born in 1897, much of my childhood was spent in an Edwardian era, an age of well ordered lives, each doing his duty in that station of life unto which it had pleased Almighty God to have called him. Did not God bless the squire and his relations, and ordain all others to keep their stations?

But now that world I knew has become a nation of parasites, battening on Social Security and supplementary benefits. And what is Social Security but the states's insurance against insurrection. A hungry man is a dangerous animal.

The first symptoms of quiz mania that still grips the village are revealed in Alf Hicks' report for the History Society.

How delighted I was when our Society won the Quiz organised by the Community Council. Our three brainy members are to be congratulated: Dorothy Anderson, D. P. Nunn (Percy), the captain, and Alan Lightly.

... Looking into the village history is great fun and occupies a lot of time. My eldest son and a friend have delved into the past, traced our family back to 1702 and found that my great grandfather, James Friend, aged only 27, of Tunstal, Suffolk, was transported to Australia for 15 years and never heard of again. His crime was writing a letter threatening to burn down a farmer's house, because he was using new machinery and putting labourers out of work! He left behind four small children, one of whom, John, became a shepherd for Eppy Issacson at Gaines Hall and someone at Thurlow.

November 1987

The year's remarkable weather changes were again prompting the Editor's comment. This time the great storm that hit the South of England and East Anglia in the early hours of October 16th.

Many of the people who have recently come to live in our village must have been pleasantly surprised to see how our local farmers and others who work on the land quickly cut their way through fallen trees to give us access to nearly all roads out of Wickhambrook by 8.30 a.m. This is what we have come to expect from them: whether it is drifts of snow, pulling stranded cars out of floods (and we have had our quota of those this year!), or fallen trees. And with few exceptions, it is not only their time that they are contributing free for our benefit, but usually their diesel. We give them stick from time to time (don't forget the hedgerows!), but their invaluable aid after the great storm came at the end of a bad harvest and at a time when they were feverishly trying to catch up on drilling the seed for next year's crops.

Many of the newcomers to the village have come here to escape the pressures of modern city life and enjoy the community spirit (as exampled above) that exists here. However, an unfortunate outcome of the mass move to East Anglia is that it has pushed up house prices so high that young local people just getting married find it extremely difficult, if not impossible, to even raise a deposit for their 'starter home'. Spare a thought for them. Have any of the politicians taken time off from telling us what they are going to do about the under-privileged in the inner cities to even consider the problems of our rural underprivileged, whose ancestors going back to Saxon and even Celtic times made this land.

In no way can we blame the newcomers to our village, particularly as your Editor is one who sneaked in here 15 years ago before the rush started. As I see it, many are driven out of the towns and cities because they have become unrecognisable from the immediate post-war years, when you could walk through some of the roughest parts of London or Birmingham without danger. The 60s and 70s policy of 'self-expression' and rejection of old fashioned discipline in the schools, and the home, has now produced its crop of self-centred hooligans, white as well as black. Coupled with this, the ever open door to immigration has meant that the cities are no longer composed

118

of a homogeneous people, of a common culture, but several conflicting cultures, with all the resultant problems of friction.

Some may be shocked by my expression of the above view; now deemed to be most unfashionable by TV pundits and liberal politicians, if not even 'racist'. I make no apologies, and we should stop kidding ourselves that the situation in the cities is otherwise.

Enough of controversy: back to our patch!

. . . Readers will see from our new Hon. Secretary's report that two more long-serving stalwarts have stood down from their posts on the Wickhambrook Community Council Committee in order to let new blood have a go. They are Peter Bayman, Secretary for 20 years, and David Turner, Treasurer for 16 years. Both, we are pleased to say, are remaining on the Committee to give the benefit of their experience.

Colin Bird was elected as the new Secretary and Gerard Catton, an accountant, as Treasurer.

Elsewhere in this issue Len Rix shrewdly observes, in verse, the characteristics of some of his fellow 'original inhabitants'. They include Alice Shave; Jack Stutters, whose daily walks around the village are now getting slower; Jack Mortlock; Bill Wright; Dr Forsythe; and retired headmaster, Dennis Morris.

ON YER BIKE

At autumn time the Wickhambrook Scene is surely at its best.
To see it you can walk or drive, but I think a bike is best.
The hedges and trees are colourful on a sunny autumn day,
But so too are the characters that we meet along the way.

There's Alice Shave going to the shop with her everlasting
     smile.
Then ther'll be Jack the walker, chalking up another mile.
To the stool on the left inside the Cloak, Jolly Jack descends.
With Shacker on the right, they're like two badly matched
     book ends.

While on the long run to Clopton, an object flashes by.
'Morning', he says, as he passes and I did just catch his eye.
With glasses and a trilby and a body that's so lean, he looked
     like a cross between roadrunner and Barry Sheen.
'Morning Doctor', I reply, as he dashes up the hill.
I used to think I was quite fit, but now I feel quite ill.

At Clopton the Happy Dockings and Keith Bannister live
     there,
Keith always had the best float at our Flower Show and Fair.
Back down to the Plumbers Arms where the pram race first
     begun.

It was a trail of beer and sweat and also a lot of fun.

In the Greyhound Mr Morris plays dominoes most days.
At school if you were naughty he made you mend your ways.
Even though you were a lazy lout, a dunce, or perfect menace,
He has forgiven all of that – and you can call him Dennis.

January 1988

'Barfly' (who was to die four years later at 50) opened his column by recording the passing of Stanley Golding

It is sad to record that Stanley Golding is no longer amongst us. He was a character who amused, often informed, sometimes caused people to reflect and debate, and occasionally expressed an argument rather pungently. He was to be seen chugging his way around the village in his maroon coloured motor-car, normally going to lunch at the Cloak, where he would meet his friend and sparring partner, Jack Mortlock. Sadly, I was not to know him for long, but my life was enriched for knowing him, as were many others.

Over the page was this entry. A tribute to five unknown young people of the area.

Lilly wishes to thank the late Mr Stanley Golding's friends for the practical help they gave him during his last few months. *(A friend of his deceased elder daughter she had come to look after him).*

She also wishes to thank the four unknown young people who pulled her car out of the ditch, after it skidded on ice, when she had to rush from Mr Golding's cottage shortly before his death in order to fetch the doctor. Last, but not least, she would also like to thank the young lady who stopped in her car whilst the above rescue was going on and who then made the call to the doctor.

March 1988

Positive action is about to take place on the development of the six acres adjoining the existing recreation ground. Peter Bayman announces that a generous local businessman, David Rowlinson of Farley Green, has offered the services of his company to prepare the ground free of charge. This entails pushing the top soil on one side and bringing the level of the field up to that of the existing recreation ground. Hundreds of lorry loads of sub-soil will have to be brought in.

TRANSPORTED FROM SUFFOLK

The History Society reported that Richard Deeks of Glemsford had given a talk on 'Transportation'.

He had spent a year in research on the subject and revealed that 2,000 males and some females from Suffolk had been transported to Botany Bay, Australia, and also Tasmania during the 19th century.

120

He has the records tabulated of every town and village in Suffolk, together with lengths of sentence of those transported, the dates of sailings and the names of the ships. He gave an horrific account of their treatment when they got there, although some did not, being drowned in shipwrecks. Punished for the least little thing, with 200 lashes being the minimum administered, it was certainly a tough life.

Thirty-eight were transported from Glemsford, Richard's village, which was more than Haverhill (a small town). Eight were transported from Wickhambrook, one for stealing a duck and a drake!

May 1988

There was another connection with transportation in Jack Mortlock's account of one of the folk tales of West Suffolk.
Some readers will have seen, many more will have heard, of the gypsy boy's grave at Kentford. This is on the old Newmarket to Bury road, at an isolated cross-roads. The boy committed suicide in the early 1800s after falsely being accused of sheep stealing. The punishment, if guilty, at that time would have been transportation for life or the gallows.

His burial party, using unconsecrated ground, thoughtfully chose a cross-roads site, to give the soul of the poor wretch a four way chance of escape from the devil. He is supposed by some to still haunt the place. It certainly has a rather eerie, slightly sinister, chilling feel, particularly at night. The grave is trimmed and tidy and fresh flowers are put onto it by persons unknown. Bus drivers and motorists often place small gifts and money on the grave to ensure a safe journey and good luck, especially on race days.

A superstition has it that on big race days, if a Newmarket man places flowers on the grave and a locally trained horse and jockey are taking part, he's onto a certain winner. Punters, don't say I didn't tell you!

July 1988

Alf Hicks reports on another centenary
An event which passed unnoticed by many people took place in the well known Plumbers Arms, namely the commemoration of the forming of the Wickhambrook Colt Show at a meeting there in 1888. The present Committee, some 30 strong, of what is now the South Suffolk Agricultural Show, decided to hold a centenary celebration and they chose the room in which the Association was founded.

It is interesting to know that the Wickhambrook Flower Show, which is approaching its 100 years, became part of the Colt Show. Later, the Rev. A. McKechnie being entrusted with starting and holding the first one at the back of the church. For many years members of the Committee of the Flower Show acted as stewards at the Colt Show.

September 1988

*Two items from Derek Pope's report from the Parish Council
again highlight the changes occurring.*

What a relief to see the old folk's housing project actually started.
The group of twelve bungalows is now under construction, and it is
expected that the whole project will be finished by next summer.
Several folk have been asking about becoming residents.

Do you know these jokers? Somebody's idea of a 'good laugh' is
to stand outside an old pensioner's house in the small hours of the
morning, throw stones at the window and shout. If any reader (with
a phone) should be unfortunate enough to suffer from these people
with a very warped sense of humour, please dial 999 immediately.
Then if possible keep the lights out and do not shout back.

November 1988

*The secretary, Colin Bird, explains why the Community Council
has changed to the Wickhambrook Community Association.*

The reason for changing our title was hopefully to eliminate certain
connotations associated with the word 'Council'. At times it inhibited
people, particularly from outside the village, from supporting us
financially. There have been occasions where individuals have
declined to contribute towards various funds because they thought
we were some sort of official body or local authority.

*Colin Bird then went on to report on the plans to organise the
village's first pantomime, which has since turned out to be a highly
successful annual event, with the audience coming from far and
wide.*

... Another first this year will be our Christmas production of 'Aladdin'. We have discussed having our own pantomime for some time,
and it was decided to take the bull by the horns when it became
obvious how popular the idea seemed to be. As with all pantomimes,
it will be a family show, so please get your tickets now – and the
more children the better.

*In his account of the previous month's History Society meeting,
Alf Hicks said that it brought back a sad memory for him.*

Our speaker was Jock Whitehouse who showed us 140 slides of
mainly Second World War airfields in this area, particularly Chedburgh and Stradishall, with their aircraft. He dealt especially with
some of the history of 214 Squadron, with their Wellesleys and Well-
ingtons, among their aircraft. He spoke for nearly two hours and no
one was bored.

He mentioned crashes at Hawkedon, where two girls rescued one
of the crew, and also at Wratting and Denston, and the bombing
of Newmarket and Stradishall aerodromes. A Dornier came down
practically intact at Gesysns (Wickhambrook) on land now farmed
by Mr Peter Bayman.

122

To my astonishment he showed a slide of a memorial tablet to Flying Officer V. Bagley, who with the crew went down in Holland and is buried there. That young airman, newly married with a lovely young wife, lodged with Ivy and me at Clopton, where he used to take our boys Gerald and Raymond upstairs. One morning he failed to return – a very sad day.

Mr Whitehouse has done a wonderful job and is continuing his research into the history of the wartime Suffolk airfields and especially 214 Squadron. Some members present were on the Stradishall airfield at that time.

Esme Jolland reported that in the annual Inter-Village Sports Competition, held in Haverhill, Wickhambrook had come second. They had got off to a flying start by winning the Junior Football, and followed this by winning the Senior Football competition. Other villages taking part were Steeple Bumpstead, Horseheath, West Wickham, The Camps, Clare and 'the Liverpool' of this competition, Kedington.

Meanwhile Barfly, having been coaxed out of the confines of the Plumbers Arms, observes:

The harvest has been gathered in and the latter day prairie schooners of the combine harvester variety have been put away for the year, and the fields have changed colour from gold to brown, and so another year begins.

Down at the Wraparound (*The Cloak*) the intellectual challenge is still being met at lunchtimes. Barfly counted no less than four copies of the *Daily Telegraph* on one day being pounded on the back page to complete the large crossword. Toy Boy Jack (*Mortlock*) was the leader of the gang who were swapping and trading their answers to the clues.

Billy the Bicycle Wright has retired (*from Justin Brookes*) and a party was held at the Wraparound the other night to celebrate the event. No more will we see Billy mounted on his tractor chugging back to base along the A143, giving those he knows a cheery wave. We would all wish for Billy to have a long and happy retirement.

January 1989

All regular contributors were full of praise for the success of the pantomime. The editor comments:

Your Community Association has put on some excellent events during 1988, the highlight of which must surely be the pre-Xmas pantomime, Aladdin. A bunch of village amateurs turned out a really professional show, which is a reflection upon the abilities of the producer, Ken Beard in bringing out their talents.

The two characters dominating the pantomime were Crichton Bridges as a rumbustious Widow Twankey and Jim Fieldsend as an evil, scheming Abanazer.

March 1989

Having been burgled whilst he was out delivering the mail and his wife was at work, Colin Bird decided to do something about it.
Since our experience with unwelcome visitors just before Christmas, a number of people have expressed an interest in a Neighbourhood Watch Scheme, I therefore brought the subject to the attention of the Community Association Committee, and it became obvious that there is sufficient interest to be able to take the matter further. The police are keen to encourage such schemes, and will address a public meeting in order to start us off on the right track.

Thus Wickhambrook became a Neighbourhood Watch zone.

May 1989

SPANISH DONKEYS

The Editor again makes a plea for contributors to confine themselves to Suffolk and Wickhambrook and district in particular.
. . . I would point out, in my customary polite manner, that it is the *Wickhambrook* Scene we wish to report upon and although events in Tehran stimulate interest, as do the plight of suffering Spanish donkeys, please keep your comments to affairs in our own patch in the main as our purpose is to give information and viewpoints that do *not* appear in the local or national press – or on the box.

Incidentally 'Messenger' why pick on the Spanish? At least they don't illtreat children and I have never heard of a Spanish child molester!

Messenger (Colin Bird) has his own views on this, stating:
Our editor very often discreetly advises and guides the Scene's contributors on the content of their articles, and his subtle and diplomatic approach is appreciated, I am sure, by all of them. So when I was approached after the last issue and asked 'what's all this rubbish about bleedin donkeys in Spain', I obviously listened with respect. 'I don't mind you writing about donkeys mush', he said, 'just so long as they're Wickhambrook donkeys.' So with that in mind, I reluctantly decided not to write about donkeys this month.

Mrs Lesley Williams reports a great response to the reopened Wickhambrook Youth Club.
Wickhambrook Youth Club opened its doors at the Memorial Hall on 10th April with a tremendous response of 60 youngsters aged 9–16. On 17th April the attendance was again 60.

A wide range of activities is run for the children, all under the supervision of adult helpers and for the first 13 weeks assisted by Suffolk Education Authority Young Leaders.

July 1989

CARNIVAL TIME!

The editor writes:
In case you did not know, Friday July 7th sees the start of our week of festive events, culminating in the 100th Flower Show and Carnival on Saturday July 15th.

Apart from reminding readers to try and come in Victorian dress to mark the centenary, my only comment is that I can empathise with the views of Alf Hicks when he looks back in nostalgia at those Flower Show and Carnival days of an era now gone, alas, and the excitement of the annual fair. Today, the fair would not come unless you could guarantee a gate of 2,000 and 'money up front', and if they did come half those attending would consider it small fry to what they see 'on Telly' and the other half, no doubt, would be trying to work out ways to vandalise the 'dodgems'. Be that as it may, what we have got on July 15th is not bad for a village and should provide fun for all those who want to have fun!

I understand that Messrs Rowlinson's lorries will be taking July 15th off! We sympathise with the long suffering people who first had the mud on the roads and now the dust as the six acre site has been slowly built up to one level – at no cost to Wickhambrook. I am told that it should come to an end in about another month. We hope that you will eventually appreciate that the extra recreational facilities for the village make it all worthwhile.

In the Horticultural Society's 'Centenary' report Alf Hicks told us how important the fair was on flower show day when he was a boy.
The Flower Show became the highlight of the year, something we, as children, looked forward to the year long. Excitement grew as the fair arrived: we loved it! 'Stingie' Wright's steam galloping horses, the high swinging boats, etc.

As we grew up we tried our strength at ringing the bell!, as the fair man shouted: 'Mind the windows!'. But only the strongest could do it. The organ thrilled us with 'I'm Forever Blowing Bubbles', 'Tipperary', 'There's a Long, Long Trail Awinding', etc.

There were the sports, six-a-side football, the marquee in the meadow back of the church; the traction engine towing the swing boats, round-abouts etc. It got stuck every year and every year Mr Wright vowed he would never come again. But he always did.

Another event marking the centenary of the Flower Show was the recording of Radio 4's Gardeners' Question Time in the Memorial Hall on 9th March.

September 1989

THE CLOAK CLOSES

*The village was shocked, some more than others, at the news of
the closure of The Cloak by brewers Greene King. The view
of most customers was summed up in a letter to 'The Scene' by
David Tomsett.*

Wasn't it amazing how many people turned up on the 'last night' to
say farewell to Dick and Angie. A shame they did not give more
support when it really counted.

I wonder how many will now write to Greene King to complain
about the loss of such an asset to village social life. You have to
admit that The Cloak provided a different atmosphere to the other
establishments and it is the loss of choice and variety that is the
biggest shame of all.

The other side of the coin is that the Brewers seem to be omnipo-
tent, having no moral obligations to the customers who have supported them for years. They are only interested in cashing-in on the
increased site values, rather than preserving a little piece of English
history.

Barfly expressed his sorrow in verse.

Alone, forlorn, and boarded up
the proud sign severed from its pole.
No more the congas start from there,
to celebrate a good New Year
and wish much joy to Bottom Shop.
No more the corners of the bar
be graced by Billy and by Jack
whose talk was oft of yester year,
sometimes with bubbles of mock ire,
which mazed the passing visitor.
No more the cry of lady host,
'Come on my Bibsley, no more wine'.
No more smooth service done by Dick.
No red light over outer door,
which signalled from the kitchen depths
'The meal is ready, serve it now!'
The crossword gang who came at lunch
have gone to other places now:
their banter and their comradeship
no more contained within those walls,
but dispersed to other places.
This part of brewers' grandest plan,
to maximize the dividend,
leaves our village without its Cloak
and friendships made are now dispersed.

126

Jack Mortlock gave us some of the history and his personal reminiscences of The Cloak.

I am sure not only regulars and casual visitors, but ordinary people must feel a sense of loss. Having been closely connected with the place for over 25 years, ten as landlord and the rest as a piece of the furniture, I was particularly sad.

Now allow me to put one or two observations to you. They are the sort of things you always wanted to know but 'was afraid to ask'.

The Cloak was unique. It was the only pub of that name in the Country, how it got its name is untraceable. I have a list of landlords with their years of occupation – going back to the early 1800s. In those early days it was also a butcher's shop. I have seen a newspaper cutting reporting that the son or employee of the landlord was on a charge of selling stolen or illegal ewe meat. That was a serious charge, the penalty for stealing a sheep was hanging or transportation for life.

Greene King took The Cloak over in 1921. Until that time beer was brewed on the premises. The brewing equipment was still there during my time: three oak mash tubs marked Nos 1, 2 and 3 Tuns; the measuring rods, copper ladles, thermometers, etc. A little room upstairs in the brew house was marked in Old English writing 'Hop Room'.

In the last century, 'ale houses' such as The Cloak were known as a Tom and Jerry – a cat and mouse existence perhaps? The person in charge, almost always a woman, wore a blue and white striped apron, like a butcher's apron and was known as a tub-woman. The husband usually had another job. When I went to The Cloak the landlord was listed as a publican ratcatcher. My grandfather who kept Stradishall Hound was a publican horse dealer and slaughterer. My uncle at the Walnut Tree in Attleton Green was a publican dealer; the man at the Greyhound a publican thatcher, and at the Depot, Ashfield Green, a publican coalman.

The Cloak is very much older than many people realised. The lounge bar and kitchen are the oldest parts of the house. Mr Bailey our local builder, who did renovations after the war, reckoned it to be one of the oldest places he had worked on, and he had done work at Badmondisfield Hall and Giffords Hall. He rebuilt the lounge fire-place with Jacobean bricks. The originals were taken away and dumped – they were hand-made, dating back to the Middle Ages. He tells me that he wishes he could remember where they were dumped. They are now worth a small fortune.

The inside of the chimney was beamed, so it was necessary at times to slap a bit of mud or plaster on those beams to prevent burning or charring. At the top a straight hole out; no brick chimney or chimney pot.

127

During the war, the lounge bar, a separate room at that time with a piano, was the meeting place of the bomber crews from Stradishall. They used to 'whoop it up' both before and after raids on Europe. If they lost a friend during a raid their rank and name with the date would be written on or between the beams. There were lots of them, often accompanied by rude comments – such as F/Sgt Dusty Miller RNZAF over Berlin November 1943 – 'you had it mate' – 'poor bastard' – or words to that effect. After the war the beams were cleaned off and relaid and repainted in between. They ought to have been left.

During my time there a New Zealander and his wife and an Australian with his wife at separate times came on a visit to England and made a special visit to The Cloak, just to see the names of their old comrades. They of course went away disappointed.

During the latter part of my time at The Cloak, I lived there alone, a position not many people envied. The building has many beams, creaking floors and stairs, and then a wooden shingle roof. After very warm days, when the building is contracting during the cool of the evening, there are many strange noises: creaking, groaning, banging and ticking. With rather more imagination than I have, one could easily believe that one is not alone.

At about this time a woman ghost-hunter, together with reporter and photographer from one of the local papers, came to investigate my ghost. They had heard somewhere of the little old lady in white. I was interviewed, photographed and the ghost-hunter had feelings – unfortunately not for me. I treated all this as a bit of a joke. I said that on going to bed at night I always looked around for the lady in white, but hadn't been lucky enough to catch her yet. The story appeared in the local press. Unfortunately I've lost my copy.

The little lady in white reputedly used to sit in the armchair in the corner of the lounge bar with her back to the road: more so when it was a separate room. Lady members of my family have said they saw and felt things. I have noticed ladies sit in that particular chair and after a while they say they are uncomfortable and move to another chair. I have on several occasions been asked at the bar: 'What happened to that little old lady that was sitting in the corner when we came in? We didn't see her leave?' She was no trouble really. She did not even occupy a seat if anyone else needed it. The only thing was, she didn't buy many drinks.

Thus ends the story of The Cloak. An historic old inn, with warmth, good conversation, humour, laughter – sometimes hilarious, but also a place of relaxation where one could sit quietly and rest awhile and enjoy its ancient charm.

Further sadness in this issue was the Editor's report of the death of Les Hurrel, whose connections with the area went back several generations.

Born and bred in Wickhambrook, Les Hurrel only had a year in retirement to share with his loving wife, Marie, to whom we extend our deepest sympathies.

As we mark the 50th anniversary this month of the outbreak of the Second World War and all its terrible consequences, it is fitting that we should also remember those who served. Les Hurrel was typical of several in this village who went off to war and was one of the fortunate ones who came back. His war was in 'small ships' of the Royal Navy which saw considerable action escorting merchant vessels in the North Sea. Not well known is that for this part of his Service he received the Naval Silver Medal. Then in 1943 he was on HMS *St Elstan*, a corvette, escorting Arctic convoys to Russia (at the age of 19). The ship was repeatedly dive-bombed and under threat from U-boats. Last year the Russian Government belatedly recognised the help given them by the RN, and Les was one of the recipients of a Russian medal.

One night in 1946, and in civvy street, Les was down The Cloak and met a young German girl who had come over here to work and could not speak a word of English. Her name was Marie, and she became Les's wife. There is a message here, however poignant, at this time of the 50th Anniversary of WW2. Les had served his country and his argument was with the German political system and not the German people as a whole.

Mrs Dorothy Anderson of the History Society gave an account
of the meeting addressed by Peter Northeast, Secretary of the
Suffolk Local History Society on the subject of Church Courts.
More than 300 years ago there was a complex system of spying, where the Bishop could find out what was happening in each parish. No one was safe, including the vicar, churchwardens, etc: all could be reported. Members were intrigued to learn that although the parishioners of Cowlinge, Stradishall, Stansfield and others amongst our neighbours were guilty of lechery, having children out of wedlock, fornication and the like, Wickhambrook people were either very good, or their spies were not doing their duty, as no mention was found of our village.

November 1989

Much correspondence, some of it acrimonious, had been roused
by the landfill operations to develop the additional six acres of
recreation ground, requiring raising the level at its lowest point
by 18 feet. Although this was carried out free of charge by
David Rowlinson, there were those who objected mainly because
of the dirt and dust on the road, and others suggesting that he
was actually making a big profit by tipping unwanted sub-soil
and hardcore. John Long pointed out that a study had been made
several years earlier and it was estimated that it would have cost

£30,000 to level the area. A full account of the cost of the operation was submitted by Mr Rowlinson, and published in 'The Scene'. It appeared that it cost him £70,000 to bring the infill material to the recreation area.

There were no comments, or letters of condolence, when that part of Mr Rowlinson's business became a victim of the recession in 1991 and was wound up.

THOSE MAGNIFICENT MEN IN THEIR FLYING MACHINES

Another contentious issue, which also hit the front page of the local papers, was the flying of microlights from a Wickhambrook base. The base was an old barn on the Claydon's farm where Frank Claydon and a couple of other enthusiasts would take off on fine days. A petition was organised for villagers to sign who opposed the microlight base, particularly on the grounds of noise and intrusion of privacy. Understandably, Frank Claydon and friends produced a counter petition stating that microlight flying from his 'strip' would be restricted to a maximum of three, and all microlights confirm rigidly to CAA regulations. There would definitely be no 'acrobats' over the village. Frank Claydon's petition received majority support. It seemed they agreed with Barfly's viewpoint.

The other day a well prepared and printed softener arrived with a thud on my doormat. The contents proclaimed an opposition to a planning application for 'Continued use of a building and land for microlight flying.' ... Firstly there is a bland statement that 'microlight aircraft are extremely noisy'. This would appear to be hypocritical hyperbole. They are less noisy than the crack of doom made by the Tornado aircraft of the RAF which 'frequently fly low over or near residential property, thereby invading individuals' privacy.'

... What about the noise the worthy burghers make with their power mowers at weekends?

... Thirdly, having read a reliable newspaper for a number of years, Barfly has not seen 'almost weekly' reports of microlight crashes – he would be grateful for more details. The thing that is disturbing is that there is an assumption which is implied that military machines have a precedence. Surely in any free society the citizen has the right to use the sky, just as he may play Pooh Sticks on the bridges over the Wickhambrook rather than have it reserved for Royal Naval submarines?

There are some who take enjoyment from seeing microlight aircraft wafting like colourful butterflies during a summer's evening, and providing the site and use does not extend to become a huge commercial operation, where is the harm?

March 1990

'Good News – Bad News' was the heading to the editorial

The bad news for many readers will be the fact that although two world wars did not stop it, in 1990 there will not be a Wickhambrook Carnival day. This is not the fault of your Community Association Committee, who have been put in a no-win situation, but due to the fact that the six acres development enters a new phase this spring with the levelling off of the ground from the new raised area, across the existing recreation ground and football pitch, right up to the Pavilion. I will say no more than let us hope it will all soon be ready and that the Pavilion can be used more frequently in the role for which it was built.

On to good news, and that is that after his successful heart pacemaker operation, Fred Thearle is 'nearly back to normal', according to his wife Maggie. Former Wickhambrook postman (the original 'GPO Flying Squad'), operator of 'The Scene' duplicator as well as putting all the pages together in company with Maggie, Editor of the 'Wickhambrook What's On', and member of the Community Association Committee, Fred has put in a lot of work for the village. I personally will send him a box of long life batteries for his pacemaker at Christmas so that he will continue to cheer me up when I see him for many years yet.

It is neither good news or bad news for Derek Bryant, who is still waiting the outcome of his appeal against St Edmundsbury Council's decision to stop him using the parking facilities on his own land at Doctor's Barn, Cloak Lane, for his two lorries. Derek wishes to thank all those local people who have supported him in his appeal.

For the record, Derek's small haulage firm has been operating from the site since 1939, when it was founded by his father. Furthermore, 'Whites Directory' in Bury Records Office shows that the same property was used as a carriage business since before 1912, when it belonged to the Pettitt family. Mrs H. M. Bryant was a Pettitt.

The main opposition to Derek Bryant continuing his small haulage business from his own property (all immediate neighbours had no objections) was a newcomer to the village, who has since moved on. This person must have had some good connections on the Council, because Derek Bryant's appeal was rejected.

Elsewhere in this issue Alf Hicks gave us further recollections of his younger days, particularly related to the two world wars.

I cannot remember the start of the Boer War, but I do remember where I was when the 1914–18 and the 1939–45 wars started.

Also, I remember King George V coming to Wickhambrook in 1912. I was five and I can picture him now standing on the school steps. He had tea in the school and a tablet was unveiled by Algenon Gardner of Denston Hall. The King was reviewing the troops. The villages were swarming with khaki-clad figures and the King was in

131

army uniform, and Sir Douglas Haig was also in the vicinity. A few frail aeroplanes floated around. (*It is alleged that during his visit King George V also drank tea in 'Workhouse Cottages', where the author now lives.*)

Anyway, it was a prelude to August 4th 1914, when war broke out and Germany invaded little Belgium.

On that day I was sitting under a huge oak tree – over 20 ft round and still there – at Home Farm with a lot of farm men who had agreed to do Mr Fuller's harvest. They had taken the one shilling which bound them to see the job through, but then they learned that war had started. A number of them were what was known as Militia men, ready for call up. Do you know, they seemed quite pleased and caring nothing for William Fuller's harvest. Sad to say, some of them never saw that Christmas. They were killed at Mons. Some were captured. My uncle, Harry Hicks, was captured with others, including the Foreman brothers of Cowlinge, and they spent four years in Germany as prisoners.

It is interesting to recall that, with Germany already in Belgium, men from Wickhambrook had to walk to Bury to join up.

I well remember Zeppelins coming over on starlit nights. They looked like cigars in the sky, and I remember that bombs fell on the Butter Market in Bury.

When the Second World War started I was with Cliff Bennington on a milk round for Justin Brooke of Wickhambrook in Shelford Road, Cambridge. As we drank a cup of tea at a cafe we heard Neville Chamberlain on the wireless say: 'It is the evil things we shall be fighting.'

DYING OF HUNGER

Harry Mott of Lidgate, in what was to be his last contribution to 'The Scene', continued Alf's theme by writing of his boyhood days just after the First World War.

At the end of the 1914–18 war we lived in one of the Leys Cottages (now demolished) at Lidgate. I was to go to Rowlands Mill to buy corn for our chickens and bran for the tame rabbits, a stone of each. I had been to Hurrels shop a few times but not beyond. My instructions were to go over the cross-roads and I would see the mill about a mile away to the east. On the right just before the school was a small grocer's shop; closed, shuttered and abandoned. Over the shop was the name 'Hartley', which rang a bell in my mind. When I was a mere toddler Hartley came to our door booking orders for T. R. Woolard. I used to watch him climb on to his bicycle via the back wheel. One day he dropped a little parcel of rich fruit cake neatly wrapped in grease proof paper. Could have been his lunch or possibly a sample to show for orders.

When I arrived at the mill a stiff breeze was blowing, turning the mill sails at a fast speed, almost sweeping the ground. I had a little cart, a Tate & Lyle sugar box mounted on discarded pram wheels. The miller had seen me and came hurriedly round, afraid I might get my cart caught up in the flying sails. I was only nine years old and small for that. He shouted a warning but he was kind and invited me up to the wheelhouse. I was delighted with the creaking, groaning and swaying of the mill, like a ship on an ocean swell. The miller, his eyebrows and clothes white with flour-dust, shaded his eyes with his hand, gazing across the village like an old sea captain. When I paid the miller he gave me a penny for myself.

Having been taught war-time thrift I resolved to take the penny home for my money box. I would pass two shops selling sweets on the way home. I had had little breakfast and felt the early pangs of hunger as I passed the first shop (Woolards). By the time I climbed the hill to Wickhambrook School I sat by the school gardens and wondered how long before one died of hunger. I had read of famous explorers dying of hunger and I certainly thought I was.

I reached the second shop (Hurrels). I dare not risk trying to make it home, but I was equally scared of going into the shop. The shopkeeper's teenage daughter managed the shop. She was a few years older than myself.

Sophisticated, bobbed and shingled in the post-war hair style, she was dressed to lure young men into the shop to buy sweets or cigarettes. No 'Brute' or 'Tramp' in those days. It was Ashes of Roses or Violets or Jasmine. I had seen the girl at the back door when calling for paraffin burning oil. I had a secret childish crush on her which made me shy of going in. However, hunger drove me into the shop. I asked for biscuits, but she said they were two pence a packet. She was very kind and suggested butter sweets and locust beans, halfpenny worth of each. The sweet pod of the locust bean was sometimes fed to sheep and cattle. I wondered if these were the husks fed to the swine in the story of the Prodigal Son. I was familiar with the Bible stories and my thinking often went along biblical lines. John the Baptist survived in the wilderness on locust beans and wild honey. I had tasted wild honey and though dark and gritty I preferred it to some of the cheap dark treacle we sometimes had for spread.

My pennyworth gave me new strength and thus I lived to tell the tale.

May 1990

The levelling of the six acres is now complete, and the editor gives thanks.

There is no denying that the work on raising the level of the six acres now added to Wickhambrook's recreational ground caused inconvenience to many people. But that is now behind us and we can celebrate the marriage of the six acres to the existing recreation field!

In doing so let us extend a thank you to those who have had to take a lot of stick, but have pushed on to see the job now virtually completed. That is the Six Acres Development Committee. People enjoying the outstanding recreational facilities that Wickhambrook will offer from next year on will have them to thank. Let us also extend our thanks to Rowlinsons for enabling the work to be completed without charge to us.

Lesley Williams reports on a well commended activity of the Youth Club.

Saturday 7th April was our first litterpick and we were pleased to see 23 children arrive, some with carts. Armed with gloves and litter bags, they proceeded to do the opposite to what is normally expected from them. All the so-called 'Youngsters of Today' worked really hard, behaved impeccably and gathered approximately 25 bags of rubbish from around the village.

After the litterpick we all gathered in the Greyhound garden for lemonade and crisps with a free raffle for a £5 gift voucher. And there wasn't an empty crisp bag to be seen!

July 1990

The follies of the Poll Tax (Community Charge) had been the subject of much village comment – as elsewhere in the land. The editor adds his 'two pennorth'.

... Have you noticed that once again it is the rural areas who have to pay that little bit extra? This is the additional few pounds for the Parish Council precept. It makes as much a nonsense of the Community Charge as it did of the old rates system in that we pay a small percentage extra than those who live in Bury or Haverhill, for example, but receive considerably less in the way of services.

Then there is the new Standard Business Rate which is forcing village shops and pubs to close up and down the country as their turnover, and hence profit, is not enough to pay all the taxes. In regard to our own shop (plus post office and garage), the extra few pence they might charge compared to the supermarkets is surely recovered on the petrol (or diesel) and wear and tear saved by not driving to the supermarkets. As Alf Hicks says elsewhere in this issue in regard to our shop, 'Use it or lose it'. Similarly with our pubs. Remember The Cloak.

It would seem that whatever party is in power, the politicians' main concern is in head counting: and there are nine heads that live in the towns and cities to every one in the villages. So they don't really give a fig for that 10 per cent in the villages and even have the cheek to get you to pay £9 a head each year to be allocated to the welfare of the inner cities! If the truth be known, half the newcomers to

Wickhambrook came here to escape from that inner city way of life – now they subsidise it!

Above all, the new extra taxes make it even more difficult for young people, born in the area to live here. This is on top of the astronomical cost of buying a house that we have discussed on this page before. At least in the Nunnery Green development we have a few starter homes for rent. Let us hope there will be more – and allocated to local young people only.

A report is given of a presentation to Harold Burton for his work for the village since coming to Wickhambrook from the Fens 45 years ago.

Representatives from many organisations gathered in the Pavilion of the Memorial Hall at the end of May for a surprise reception (organised by David Turner) given to Mr Harold Burton. Harold, who has not been too well of late, had served in all organisations represented since he came to Wickhambrook in 1945. Let into the 'secret' and also present with Harold were his wife Audrey and their sons Richard and Stephen.

David Turner welcomed them and explained the purpose of the evening. He then introduced Stuart Roebuck, currently Wickhambrook Cricket Club's leading wicket taker (and a fair bat, too). Stuart read from a diary (provided by Alf Hicks) that Harold Burton had been a great spin bowler in his time, taking 6 for 12 runs at a match on 6th June 1947 and then on July 12th of that year had scored 43. He pointed out that Harold, who is still president of the club, had been connected with its administration for 40 years. In recognition of this, the Cricket Club had decided to rename the Wickhambrook Cup the 'Harold Burton Trophy'.

Steve Williams, Captain of Wickhambrook Cricket Club, then presented Harold with two prints of portraits of 19th century cricketers from engravings by Henry Adlard.

Peter Bayman, as Chairman of the Parish Council, stated: 'We are here to show our appreciation and thanks to Harold for the outstanding interest he has shown in village affairs in the last 45 years.' He spoke of Harold's time as a player and then chairman of the Football Club and his involvement with the Memorial Social Centre from the outset in 1946.

Apart from his service as a player for Wickhambrook cricket and football, and then Chairman of both Clubs, he also served as a Parish Councillor for a number of years in the fifties.

He joined the Committee of the Horticultural Society in 1946, and ran the children's sports for the Queen's Coronation in 1953. He was President for many years, resigning in 1988. He has shown his own garden products throughout this time and won over 870 prizes. He also acted as a Show Judge at many shows in Suffolk and Cambridgeshire.

He was a founder member of the Snooker Club and is still the Secretary.

November 1990

Sad news in this issue was the report on the passing of Mrs Enid Claydon, the matriarch of the Claydon family. Well respected and a notable villager, she was in her 93rd year.

It was also reported:

We were shocked to hear of the death in America of Tony Tuten, a Sergeant in the US Airforce, who lived in Attleton Green for over two years. One of the 'quiet Americans' he was popular with the customers of the old Cloak. He liked it so much here that he chose to come back to Wickhambrook for a week's holiday last year! Only 28, we do not know how he died at present.

Elsewhere we see that quiz mania still has its hold on many. In the annual village quiz knockout, the History Society were again champions, defeating the ladies of the WI by 52 points to 45. In the Greene King Sunday Quiz League, the old Cloak team had been adopted by the Lidgate Star. Team members Alan Lightley (also the star player for the History Society), son Richard Lightley, David Tomsett and Stuart Henderson, went on to win the League for three consecutive years.

It is noted that at a well attended meeting in the Memorial Hall, the Neighbourhood Watch scheme was officially launched and is up and running, initially through the efforts of Colin Bird.

January 1991

More sad news, coupled with embarrassment for the editor

It is regretted that in the last issue of 'The Scene' there was a full page report on the Golden Wedding of the late Mr Harold Burton and his wife Audrey, after he had passed away. We sincerely apologise to Mrs Burton and her family for any additional grief this may have given them.

March 1991

The ultra-modern Doctors' surgery, serving many other villages as well as Wickhambrook, is in the capable hand of Dr Polkinhorn, Dr Lloyd-Jones (who took over from Dr John Batt when he retired) and Dr Carlton-Brown. The practice manager, Barry Carpenter, reports on its recently completed extension.

... In particular there was an urgent need for an office and clinical room for visiting health staff (health visitors, midwives, chiropodists, physiotherapists, district nurses, etc), for a fourth consulting room for the trainee doctor, for a w.c. for the disabled (and better access for them), for a larger waiting room and for more office space.

... Now that it is completed (except for one or two minor touches) we hope that you will agree that the inconvenience was worthwhile.

We are quite sure that the new facilities will enable us to provide a better service and indeed more services, such as the newly started Well Person Clinic.

It is announced that the local Boys Brigade is about to celebrate its 50th Anniversary. The announcement is signed 'Brigadier' – none other than the ubiquitous Alf Hicks.

The next two months are important ones in the history of the Company. There are two important dates and it is hoped all who can will come and celebrate with the 8th Mid Suffolk Company of the Boys Brigade for their 50th Anniversary.

... The company was actually formed at Wickhambrook on 16th March 1941. It was enrolled by Rev. H. Hewitt, Methodist Minister, who was the founder. Supporting him at the Service were Rev. W. H. Cook, vicar of All Saints Wickhambrook; Rev. William Rose, Haverhill Methodist Superintendent; and Rev. H. G. Steer, Congregational Minister. Within a year the Rev. Hewitt, the Company's first captain, moved on. He was succeeded by Mr Lewis Hurrell, who was Captain for over twenty years. Following him were Mr Ivan Peacock, Mr Dennis Plummer and Mr Norman Gardner. The present Captain is Mr John Walladge.

It is good to know that the Company, about 40 strong, is doing well at present and has revived the Drum and Bugle Band.

An item at the bottom of a page reveals the parlous state of the cricket club.

The present editor, John Bean, has been given the honour of being asked to be Chairman of Wickhambrook Cricket Club, and will therefore supply a Cricket Club report for future issues.

July 1991

Alf Hicks reports that Wickhambrook is to become the centre of a rural catchment area for sports and recreation.

With big plans ahead and promise of financial assistance by the St Edmundsbury Borough Council for sports and recreational development for the village as a centre of a catchment area, the Social Centre committee finds itself with much more to do.

However, it is believed that the way forward is bright. The village already has 23 flourishing voluntary groups and organisations. Also, a splendid Community Centre and now nine acres of recreational ground, and recently a pavilion, built mainly by voluntary labour, has been added.

Wickhambrook, hitherto termed 'ten miles from anywhere', will become the centre of roughly a five mile radius and be of benefit to some 15 smaller villages within that area. The development will take place over a ten year period and will mean organisations raising funds.

137

. . . A planning committee called RAFT (Rural Activity for the 90s) is working hard on the project. The Parish Council is playing an important part and also the local Community Council.

The Chairman of RAFT is Jeff Claydon (also a Parish Councillor), and the Secretary is Mike Elers.

Barfly has also observed the progress of the additional six acres – and also the actions of some local lads on 'high spirits'.

. . . The verdant pastures of the six acres look good, although it is a pity that in spite of herculean efforts by the organisers of the project, football will not be played there this year, which is a tragedy as it means that the younger generation will have to continue going out of the village for their recreation.

. . . Recently there was a dance at the village Memorial Hall. Judging from the discarded strong lager cans, empty strong cider bottles and empty spirit bottles discarded around the hedgerows in the vicinity of the Hall, the licenced bar could not have done as well as it might. However, the aimless packs of drunken young which maraud the locality after the event are counterproductive. This time windows of the office of the local builders were smashed by these mindless morons.

September 1991

The annual carnival receives another blow, this time as a knock-on effect of increasing UK and EC legislation.

Exhausted through arranging, preparing, participating and clearing up after the week of events, some members of the Community Association Committee felt very despondent after the Carnival. With only two floats taking part, it was the smallest number anyone can recall. However, let it be said that several organisations would have had a float, but with the high insurance and immaculate roadworthiness now required, farmers were rather reluctant to loan their trailers. Some people were also disappointed at the attendance, but in fact throughout the afternoon some 750 people came along. Trouble is that our ground is so big now that even 1000 would look sparse!

'Barfly', whose column becomes more like that of Jeffrey Bernard, was in a gloomy and even misogynistic mood. His 'brown study' was brought on by the recent case of a Dorset villager who had to dispose of his cockerel because its dawn calls awoke his new neighbour.

Once upon a time there was a man who kept a stag turkey, chickens, other fowl and geese. His family had been in the village for years, as had he. He loved his feathered friends. He and they were complimentary to one another for their well being.

Gradually the village expanded. Beautiful new bungalows and bijou houses were built. Nothing too elaborate, just little boxes, three up, two down semis, constructed of clashing red cheap brick and unseasoned timber. Gradually people arrived from all over and a new faceless community was born and suckled by the supermarkets in the nearest town. There was an influx of small motor cars for the wives to go shopping in whilst the husbands zoomed off to the big city in the Sierras, Cavaliers and Roundheads, each vehicle sporting a coat-hanger to suspend the uncreased jacket over a rear side window. They go off at 6.30 a.m., not to return until 8.00 p.m. that evening, tired out and having burnt themselves out on the motorway long before they started work. At work and in the pub at lunch time they boast of the countryside they hardly ever see.

But what of the wives? During term time they take their homogenised and pasturised offspring to the local school and kindergarten. Do the minimum of mechanicalised housework and drink coffee with their other bored clones. They discuss good works, amorous gossip and inconsequential matters ad nauseum. All this goes well until the school holidays, when the children make demanding inroads into their vapid existences.

The pigs from the nearby farm keep their brats from their afternoon sleep by their squeals, to say nothing of the smell. The combine harvesters hum their way into empty skulls thus disturbing any vestige of a thought pattern they might have. But something stirs within that hollow bone sphere: 'This is not like the countryside we grew to love pictured on the chocolate boxes – we must do something about it. We must stop the pigs squealing. We must stop the church clock chiming each quarter. We must stop those dreadful smells. We must stop those farmworkers using the local pub for something to drink to wash down their "dockie": they really are dirty you know.'

So where does this leave us and our little man with his gobblegook hens and geese? We will complain, we will compel the Environmental Health Department to make abatement orders. Thus our old man has to say goodbye to his friends – the Magistrates have made an order. However, the geese remain. Nobody has complained about them. Why? Because the complainers have seen a programme on the telly showing geese used as watch dogs in a whisky bonded store at a distillery and that spells security in this transitory and aimless world and thus they are acceptable.

Barfly's popularity amongst some ladies of the village was further diminished.

November 1991

Surprise For Mr Wickhambrook
The Editor writes:
On 27th September over 200 people turned up at the Memorial Social Centre, having been asked not to let Alf Hicks, 'Mr Wickham-

brook', know the purpose of the meeting. The secret was kept and Alf turned up, having first driven past the hall, believing that he was coming to a meeting to discuss the twinning of our village with a village in Bermuda.

The purpose of the occasion was to make a presentation to Alf for all the work he had done over the years for the village, through so many organisations. For those who were not at the meeting, or who were but could not hear the announcement over the jollity of the evening, *some* of them are as follows –

Attended the first public meeting in 1945 when it was decided to build a Memorial Hall as a War Memorial. Founder member of the Wickhambrook Community Council (now Association) in March 1967. An officer (currently Brigadier) for 49 years of the 8th Mid-Suffolk Company, Boys Brigade. A lay preacher and Sunday School Teacher of the Congregational Church for 43 years. Played football for Wickhambrook until he was 40, then a referee until his early 60s. Played for the Cricket team and then Vice-Chairman for 10 years. Member and later a Committee member of the Snooker Club since its foundation. For 35 years he was a member of the Parish Council and also served on the Executive of the Suffolk Association of Local Councils AND our most prolific contributor to 'The Scene'!

Supported by his family and many members of the Hicks-Jolland clan, Alf was in fine form, once he had got over the initial surprise. His old boyhood friend, Clement Fuller, regaled us with details of Alf's earlier life that would be befitting to a 'This is Your Life' programme, with Alf's heckling giving much amusement.

There is a short account of one of the Plumbers Arms' musical evenings.

'Artistes' ranging from seven to 70 years entertained Plumbers Arms customers on October 19th with music, songs and comedy, and raised over £67 for the Royal National Institution for the Blind.

Thanks go to the 'Artistes', Paul Coleman, Roger Dennis and Denis Hayes, with wind instruments backing from Claire Pruden, Clare Hayes and Claire Beatty. Songs and musical contributions also came from Clare Charlwood, Jim Fieldsend, Helen Wreathall, landlady Marilyn Pruden's mum (!), Kerry Robinson, and sisters Laura (10) and Claire Smith (7) from Yorkshire.

January 1992

Some words of praise for the young people of the village from one of the old folk, Mr Bill Clayton.

I would like to thank the members of the Wickhambrook Youth Club who looked after us at the Happy Hours Club annual dinner, held just before Christmas. Not only did they serve and wait upon us, but everybody commented on how smart they were.

On behalf of the pensioners in Wickhambrook I would also like to thank those Youth Club members who helped two of their organisers, Mrs Lesley Williams and Mrs Roz Clary, to deliver the free EEC butter round the village. It was all voluntary, in the ladies own busy time, with petrol supplied by Mrs Williams. It was much appreciated.

The editor comments on Bill Clayton's letter:
It is refreshing to see the letter in this issue from Mr Bill Clayton praising the members of Wickhambrook Youth Club. We know that they are not all angels – far from it, but it shows that we 'oldies' recognise them as part of our overall community.

It is also a reflection on the hard work by the organisers of the Youth Club in building up what is probably the most successful Youth Club in the History of the village.

... Of course many youngsters yearn for the bright city lights in preference to 'dull old village life', but it has its down side as well as the up. For a start, that community spirit is in much shorter supply, particularly in the big cities. Again, although at times village life may seem dull, at least it is comparatively safe to city life. But above all you can grow up here with a sense of belonging. Belonging to a community and belonging to nature's scheme of interrelationship with all the varied forms of life that surround us.

May 1992

In Trouble With The Trojan Horse
Breaking all the rules, I decided to publish an anonymous letter, because of what I considered to be its importance. It was to get me in to some trouble.

... I refer to the large area of land to the rear of the village hall which has been filled and levelled to provide extra recreational and sporting facilities. Whilst these plans appear to be of great advantage to the village, there are some related facts which I feel cast a shadow over these benefits. In order to achieve these ends a very sizeable grant has been approved by St Edmundsbury Borough Council.

First of all I do not believe that such a sum is ever provided for nothing. I am a great believer in the adage 'Beware of Greeks come bearing gifts'. And I can tell you quite categorically that unofficial but serious discussions have taken place within the Borough Council regarding large scale building development in Wickhambrook after the year 2000...

... Of course, if you were to approach St Edmundsbury they would deny such plans exist, and I can supply no documentary evidence at this time to back my claim. I simply know it to be true.

July 1992

The publication of the anonymous letter led to a ready acceptance by Mr A. R. Johnson, Borough Council Planning Officer, to address the Annual Meeting of Wickhambrook Parish Council. 'The Scene' reported:

Mr Johnson stated that they had all the land required for future development in West Suffolk and that for at least 15 years 'there would be no major development of Wickhambrook.'

John Long, the village's representative on St Edmundsbury Borough Council, gave his viewpoint on the anonymous allegations, whilst delivering a rocket to the editor for not contacting him in the first place.

Firstly I would like to make comment on the person who has not the strength to put his or her name to the article. Secondly, the article should not have been published without at first making sure that the contents had any foundation and any semblance of truth. Either myself or any member of the Planning Committee, or the Planning Officer, Mr Allen Johnson, would have given that information. It was pure conjecture on the writer's part, because the village had been given the large grant over ten years there would be strings attached. There never has been any such plan, neither in the Suffolk Structure Plan or the Borough of St Edmundsbury Plan, which covers the whole area well into the next century, as there is sufficient land in ownership by the Borough to cover all the needs of the prospective increase of population of approximately 1000 per annum.

Had I the knowledge that this article was to appear last month, I would have made my reply so that it could appear in the same issue. To reply two months later is too late, and the damage is done.

Paul Saunders was also observing the changes in the village, in his first article for 'The Scene'.

I can't take you back very far in the history of Wickhambrook, only 25 years to August 1967 when my family moved from London and bought the village store. The move was recommended by my father's doctor, who insisted the country air would be good for him. Maybe it was, but it only bought him another four years.

I arrived in Wickhambrook as a young and impressionable teenager, with all the Townie's preconceptions. I thought it was a huge, free playground, where you could walk anywhere you pleased, ride horses all over the place and do pretty much anything you felt like. It wasn't, although it was a great deal more liberated than it is today.

Kids make friends easily, and within a couple of months I was well in with the local 'tearaways', a word I use guardedly, because the idea of real tearaways simply doesn't fit with the Wickhambrook of the late sixties at all. We used to do some daft things, but we nearly always got away with it and by some miracle we're all still alive! I

142

can honestly say we had a great deal of fun without doing anybody any real harm.

The whole atmosphere of the place was completely different. I suppose it's fair to say the rest of the world hadn't caught up with Wickhambrook at the time, or perhaps vice versa! It was one of the largest villages in Suffolk, but with one of the smallest populations. What housing there was being ancient, spread out and in many cases very dilapidated.

The pubs were an education, although I had to wait until I was nearly fifteen before being allowed in openly! All three were small and poky, with open fires roaring away and the atmosphere heavy with character. It's not like that now. Don't get me wrong, I still enjoy a drink in the Plumbers or the Greyhound and I'm not averse to change, but physical change often creates social change, and that isn't always for the best.

Development in Wickhambrook, by and large, has been done well. It is still largely unspoilt, which is more than you can say about the indiscriminate development which has gone on in some villages I could name. Along with new housing, the old has been preserved, something which happens all too rarely. Few of those who complained loudest when 'City folk' bought up the ruined houses and refurbished them as weekend cottages could stand with their hand on their heart and say the result degrades the appearance of the village.

How it affected the social structure is another matter entirely. There are those who say change is welcome and necessary, and others who declare it unwelcome but unavoidable. I wouldn't like to declare allegiance to either side, preferring to see good and bad in both arguments, but there's no doubt the village has changed.

The pressures society places on everyone to succeed has spilled from the towns and cities out to the villages, and the general result is that no one has any time to spare. Whereas people would stand in the shop and chat for hours (where, incidentally, you can pick up more information than anywhere else), now it's a question of rush in, grab what you need, and rush off again. Wickhambrook is by no means unique in this and it's true to say the village has retained its character better than most others.

Perhaps I remember it so fondly because I grew up there. It doesn't matter where you're born, the important thing being the source of education for life. I learned more from the people of Wickhambrook about how to survive than anywhere else.

The fun of being part of the village seems to have gone. It was fun, too. Where else could you saw up a few old cars, weld them into one and thrash round the fields in your own creation all day? Where else could you find a mammoth barbecue starting on a Friday night and finishing, via several other houses, the following weekend?

143

It's still a lovely place to live, and one day I hope I might be able to move back. But anybody who grew up in the village in the sixties will tell you the kids there today have no hope of having as good a time as we did. They can't, because they are a product of a different type of rural society.

September 1992

This issue gave readers the sad news that Jack Mortlock and Maggie Thearle had died suddenly the previous month. Jack's sons Tony, Chris and Peter Mortlock gave a summarised account of their father's interesting, and even intriguing, life, much of which has already been given in the introduction to this Suffolk Chronicle. They recognised his valuable and often humorous contributions to 'The Scene', which the editor would sorely miss in the quest to try and achieve the right 'balance'.

His articles for 'The Scene' reflected his interest in local history, farming lore and the Suffolk dialect which he managed to lose during the course of his 40 years odyssey.

His sudden death was a shock to us all. He was a man able to communicate with people of all ages and from all walks of life and we somehow assumed he would always be here.

He will be sadly missed.

The editor's page had been stretched to two pages – most of it headed 'In Memorium'. It also recorded the death of Bernard Jolly – Wickhambrook born and bred, who served on destroyers during the war, as well as Jack Mortlock and Maggie Thearle.

Perhaps the greatest shock was the death of Mrs Maggie Thearle. She came to this village with husband Fred (our former postman) over 25 years ago and was a teacher for a time at the Wickhambrook Primary School. With Fred, she joined the Community Association Committee some 15 years ago, was the promoter for seven years and right up until she went into hospital she covered *three* rounds as a collector for members subscriptions to the Community Association and delivering the copies of 'The Scene'. Her physical and mental energies – as Committee members would often find – would put many a 30-year-old in the shade. Maggie Thearle was also a former President of Wickhambrook WI and even appeared on the Hall stage as Piglet (with the editor as Christopher Robin) in 'Winnie the Poo', one of Peter Bayman's Christmas carol concerts.

Village life was still continuing, with a great day for the Cricket Club, playing at home for the first time in three years.

... The Club was able to have an official opening of the new pitch on the enlarged recreation ground. The occasion was made into an all day Six a Side Knockout in which six teams: Wickhambrook, Stradishall, Stansfield, Gazeley, Cheveley and a combined Ousden and Lidgate team took part.

...Wickhambrook and Stradishall emerged as the finalists, with Stradishall being the winner.

...Mrs Audrey Burton was asked to present a silver Challenge Cup given by the Club and to be called the Harold Burton Trophy in memory of her husband. Mrs Burton congratulated the winners and presented the trophy to the Captain, Mark Jolland. The rest of the team included his two brothers, James and Nicholas *(The three Jollands are Wickhambrook lads)*. The runner-up team, Wickhambrook, was Stuart Roebuck, Darren Williams, Scot Williams, Mark Denley, Ian Pollard and Dave Lawson.

Other sports clubs were blossoming with the advent of the extended recreational ground.

The Tennis, Bowls and Petanque Clubs are holding a joint Open Day to mark the official opening of the tennis courts, the success of the bowls practice area, and the inauguration of the Wickhambrook Petanque Club's local terrain . . . There will be a full lunchtime barbecue and an all-day 'refreshment' tent.

November 1992

The Editor reports on a meeting organised by the Rural Activities For The Nineties (RAFT 90s).

Scene readers would have been very impressed at the efficiency of RAFT 90s in co-ordinating the expenditure of the various clubs in a manner that is enabling them to obtain the maximum grand aid from the Borough Council. In its two years existence the RAFT Committee's account shows transactions totalling in excess of £75,000. £36,000 has been raised by the various sports and leisure clubs as cash or labour equivalent, working through the co-ordination of RAFT 90s, with the balance being grant aid from the Borough!

...As RAFT works closely with the MSC Hall Committee, perhaps next year they will have a word with them about a suitable location for the November 5th bonfire site. As readers will know, due to the unfortunate illness of Peter Bayman – I hear he is on the mend – this year's fireworks had to be cancelled. If the event had gone ahead though, the site allocated would have meant that for safety reasons it would not have been possible to also have a bonfire. Remember, this is not a 'minority event'. A thousand people turn up for our Bonfire Night.

Unfortunately for many this was the end of the now legendary fireworks displays put on by the Community Association every November 5th. With Peter Bayman as MC, and also often making a personal donation to the cost, it was one of the largest displays organised by a Suffolk village and drew crowds from many miles around. The Youth Club now puts on a smaller – but growing – fireworks display.

145

A small item tucked away at the end of this issue reminds us that burglaries are now commonplace.
With a spate of burglaries in Wickhambrook and the surrounding area recently, and reports of suspicious phone calls thought to have been made to determine whether the house was occupied, there is a special need to be watchful.

January 1993

THOUGHTS OF A FAILED RAT CATCHER
The editorial of this issue, under the above title, has since assumed greater significance as the majority city and suburban dwellers embrace the Bambi Syndrome.
Over the New Year I spent some hours in trying to kill a rat who had come from a nearby compost heap to nose round my door. My now aging cat, who in her youth would kill anything that moved as long as it was not more than twice her size, went through all the motions but didn't even score a near miss. Surprising to me, the only creature to *nearly* get the rat was a cock pheasant, who apparently objected to the rat going for his jugular.

I got to thinking. If that rat had a nice fluffy tail and his face was not so pointed, people would call me a monster for wanting to despatch him not only from my lawn but from this earth. Now, if I had shot the pheasant, quite a number of people would also consider me a monster. Perhaps city-based Animal Rights activists would demonstrate in Wickhambrook, such is the dominance of emotion over common sense when it comes to the relationship of homo sapiens with the rest of the animal kingdom.

Like the rest of my species, I was born an omnivore, i.e. I need a diet of meat and two veg. Although I would find it difficult to kill a pheasant, I would if hungry, but certainly not for 'sport'. To me, there is a world of difference between shooting a pheasant or two for 'the pot' and trying to outdo each other in seeing how many you can slaughter, to give away, in one afternoon. Yet again, pheasants are so stupid that if they were not reared for shooting, their natural predators – including the fox – would have probably eliminated them in Britain by now.

Then what of Brer Fox himself? If he had a rat-like tail instead of such an attractive brush would 'anti-Hunt' protestors be so keen to throw themselves under horses hooves? We won't go into the equally emotive issue of the carnage the fox can cause in a chicken run, but point out that ten times as many foxes are killed by the motor car than by huntsmen. And the hunt is certainly a quicker way than snaring or shooting, which often leads to a lingering death.

I do not hunt, but respect the rights of those who want to. All I

146

say is that if Brer Fox had gone to earth, he has won – that's his rights.

Obituaries in this issue included that of Miss Alice Shave, whose lifetime, stretching back to before the First World War, had been spent in Shop Hill, Wickhambrook. Also, Mrs Helen Long, wife of Councillor John Long. A lady with a great sense of humour, she was for many years the Treasurer of the Memorial Social Centre Committee, a founder member of the Community Council Committee and a long serving member and of course, at one time the Mayoress of Bury St Edmunds.

An item at the foot of a page was headed 'Vandals In Wickhambrook'.

Why is it that whilst there are a lot of very decent teenagers about there are a small minority who go around damaging cars and property in the Nunnery Green and Croft Close area of our village? At least three cars have been damaged and garden property upset. However, the Police, who have plenty of far worse problems, are doing their best and have their suspicions of one or two persons. There could be developments.

May 1993

Praise is given to Mr Jack Stutters, known as the 'walking man of Wickhambrook', and who is also the church bell ringer.

Special mention is made by the Vicar, the Reverend W. Davis, of a very faithful member of the church and one who must be known to almost everyone in Wickhambrook: Mr William (Jack) Stutters. William, he says, is well loved and a familiar figure who keeps fit by walking. He has often been offered lifts, but always refuses them.

A remarkable man. When you hear those bells ringing at 8 o'clock on Sunday morning it is William in action; always punctual and having walked half a mile.

Also, at 78 years he still climbs the 34 stairs up the belfrey to wind up, with both hands, the two very heavy weights twice a week to keep the clock going. This clock was placed as a memorial in 1946 to those who fell in the 1939–45 war.

It was decided that William should have some recognition for performing this task for 40 years – and still going strong, so on Mothering Sunday a presentation was made to him with a card bearing the signatures of all present.

July 1993

BRING IN THE NEW EDITOR

In this issue I announced that I was to retire from editing 'The Scene' after eighteen and a half years. Without contrivance, my last editorial ended on what was to be a note of controversy.

. . . In thanking our readers and advertisers for their support we must also thank our contributors past and present. Outstanding amongst these is Alf Hicks. What will we do if *he* retires? I hope our new editor, Jim Fieldsend (of pantomime and Plumbers Arms quiz fame) can read Alf's writing! Another contributor, Barfly (Bernard Young), has been very ill in hospital but is now on the mend having been fitted out with a new liver. We hope he does not abuse it or Addenbrookes Hospital might ask for it back.

During my stint I have raised a few controversial issues, some right, some wrong. One of these was the extraordinary decision of St Edmundsbury planners that led to Derek Bryant having to cease running his haulage business from his own land at Doctor's Barn, Cloak Lane, which was started there by his grandfather 60 years ago. Well, the best of luck to the new people who have now built a house on the land, and whilst nobody wishes to criticise them in any way, how is it that they can operate their vans for their tiling business from that site?

Meanwhile the Plumbers Arms A Quiz team was able to record an outstanding success.
In the Greene King IPA Masterquiz the Plumbers Arms A team reached the finals for the whole of the Greene King area – some 350 pubs stretching from Kent to Bedford to Norfolk. After beating the 'Victoria' from Hitchin, they finally became runner-up to the 'Goat & Boot' of Colchester.

The Plumbers Arms A team on the finals night consisted of Peter Docking, Jim Fieldsend, John Bean, with Marilyn Pruden (Landlady of the 'Plumbers') standing in for regular team member Maggie Pearson of Ousden. Other team members, who played an important part in the League games which got the team into second place and into the knockout playoffs for the finals included Richard Beighton, Heinz Seiler and Bernard Young (Barfly).

This issue was also to report the untimely death of Bill Dyer, in his mid-fifties, captain of The Greyhound quiz team. Of Scottish origin, he and his wife had lived in the area for 30 years. A man with a great sense of humour, he thought life was for living and not for vegetating.

Much interest has been shown in Wickhambrook's 1859 letter box, one of the oldest in the country, with people coming from far and wide to photograph it. Located at Boyden End, it had become surplus to GPO requirements. Alf Hicks reports:
Representatives of Newmarket and Cambridge GPO have now been out and met with the Parish Council and members of the local History Society. As a result the Postal Authorities and the Parish Council will work together and decide what to do. They appreciate the Jones family being willing to have the pillar box on their property. Another idea of the Parish Council is to have the ancient box removed and

resited near the Old Farmstead on Moor Green near the Greyhound, then remove the present, more modern, letter box near the chapel at Meeting Green.

September 1993

Sadly, Barfly (Bernard Young) had paid the ultimate price for too many visits to too many bars. It was given to the new editor, Jim Fieldsend, to write his obituary.

It was in the early spring of 1987 that I first met Bernard following my posting to Highpoint Prison, where he was an Assistant Governor. Over the next few years I not only worked with him behind the fence but was a founder member of the Plumbers Arms B quiz team with him. Bernard was a veritable mine of useless information. He had an extensive knowledge of the British Railway system, an encyclopaedic knowledge of the pubs and hostelries of England and was completely up to date with the goings on in Coronation Street.

He had a chequered career which included a commission in the Life Guards and being a salesman for Lyons cakes, all of which eventually led him to the Prison Service. After almost twenty-five years service, Bernard was medically retired last April. Following two failed liver transplants he died in the operating theatre on the 6th July whilst receiving a third.

His funeral service at Wickhambrook Parish Church was attended by many of his former Governor colleagues and a guard of honour was formed by the uniformed staff from Highpoint. His sense of humour did not fail him, even at the end – I am quite sure that Bernard was sitting on the rain cloud turning on the tap over that guard of honour.

Gill Corbyn, Secretary of the Community Association, tells of the success of this year's Carnival Day.

Carnival Day was certainly warmer and drier than last year but unfortunately a storm left a lot of the procession cold and rather damp. Weren't the floats superb this year? We all thought the entries were fantastic, especially when you looked closely at the detail on each vehicle. We congratulate all the entries, but particularly the Dumbo float which was entered by the Welsh and Joplin families. What an effort from two households! The stalls all seemed to be making a healthy profit for the people concerned.

Miss Wickhambrook, Danielle Williams, with her princesses, Marie Lathangue and Elizabeth Edwards, led the parade, marshalled by Parish Council Chairman Peter Bayman, as it toured the village.

Steam Boat Bill entered by Wickhambrook School won the Len Harbut Silver Bowl with the Playground's 101 Dalmations second.

November 1993

Jim Fieldsend, as editor, gave details of the plans of the Memorial Trust Fund for RAF Stradishall – now the location of Highpoint prison.

This has started with a display, talk and slide show given by members of the Trust, a group of local enthusiasts who have spent fourteen years gathering memorabilia, photographs, original records and historical facts associated with the airfield during its 32 operational years.

A strange quirk of fate led to it being called 'Stradishall' as it is after all mostly in the parish of Hundon. But the name 'Stradishall' was used to ensure that it was not confused with RAF Hendon in North London.

On Sunday 10th October a Memorial Service and dedication of a stained glass window commemorating those who died (640) whilst serving at the airfield was held in the parish church of St Margarets in Stradishall.

I wonder what those gallant men who gave their lives would make of the present incumbents of Stradishall Camp. Not a lot, I would think.

January 1994

The death is announced of Wickhambrook-born character, Victor Harrod, nick-named 'Chatty'.

The death has occurred in the West Suffolk Hospital, Bury St Edmunds, of a very well known personality, a real Suffolk character, Victor Charles Harrod. In his 80th year, he did a lot for the Parish Council, on which he served for 40 years. He was also on Clare Rural District and St Edmundsbury Councils for ten years. He also did a lot of work, including collecting thousands of pounds, for the benefit of the children, particularly for their play area on the recreation ground.

During the war he served under General Montgomery in the desert. He was in the Tank Corps, and his tank commander was Baring-Gould, whose grandfather, S Baring-Gould, wrote the hymn Onward Christian Soldiers. This was Vic's favourite.

In a letter to the editor I paid my own respects to Vic Harrod.

I was saddened to hear of the death of Vic Harrod and very much regret that my work kept me away from his funeral. He and I crossed swords a couple of times in these pages, but neither of us bore any malice. He was a man who spoke his mind and one 'character' less in this conformist world. He once told me that when you had lived in Wickhambrook 21 years then you could get your Suffolk passport. I regret that in March this year he will not be around to present me with mine.

March 1994

Jim Fieldsend assures us that Wickhambrook will have a future generation or two.

... When one hears of villages dying for want of young blood, it was wonderful to see the turnout for the children's party on the 9th January. Over 50 children between three and ten turned up for fun and games, and of course tea and a gift. And if noise is anything to go by these kids will have no problem keeping Wickhambrook alive well into the next century.

Meanwhile, our local MP, Tim Yeo, was in hot water nationally for his part in contributing to the next generation, even if out of wedlock. The editor published my thoughts on this affair. Being unenthusiastic with certain views of John Major's liberal-conservative Government, I was considering withholding my vote for our local MP, Tim Yeo, at the next election. I now have two good reasons for rescinding this view.

Firstly, as editor of a trade journal covering the metal finishing industry, I found that the industry thought that there was a marked change in the Department of the Environment when it came under Mr Yeo's guidance, in that his Department took on board the comments from the Metal Finishing Association (the industry's trade association) in regard to industrial effluent problems facing the industry. This was in marked contrast to the period before he took up office.

Secondly, I object to the media usurping the function of the electorate in deciding who or who should not be Government Ministers. We may decide not to vote for Mr Yeo because his personal life hardly fits in with his party's call of 'Back to Basics'. Others may feel that his proven ability as a Minister does not conflict with that personal life, and therefore he will get their vote. We decide. Not the gutter press looking for scandal in order to boost sales.

July 1994

Readers will recall that the first extract from 'The Scene' of 25 years ago mentioned the fortunes of Wickhambrook Football Club and one or two players of that time, including Steve Jolland. Writing in this current issue John Stokes, Club Secretary and a former Captain, tells us of the outstanding success of the Club in the 1993/94 season and asks whether there has been a more successful season. Three of Steve Jolland's sons are in the team: Mark, James (Captain) and Nick.

Playing in Division II of the Mick McNeil League, the team won 25 of its 26 games, scoring 170 goals.

Roll of Honours:
    Division II Champions
    Division II K.O. Cup Winners

Mick McNeil Cup Winners
St Edwards Invitation Cup Runners up
Trophy for the most goals scored in the league
... But the talent of this team should not be underestimated. In winning the Mick McNeil cup, we disposed of three of the top four teams in Division I including the champions, Cockfield, in the final.

... There is a nucleus of young talent in this team that can only get better. The big question is, will it stay together? Should that be the case, there is no reason why the team cannot take Division I by storm in the same way they have won Division III and II in successive seasons. *(As this Chronicle goes to press the team holds top spot in Division I).*

The team has been galvanised together by Paul Smith and Jimmy Jolland and on the pitch everyone has played their part. None more so than the Jolland brothers, Mark and Jimmy. Both have played exceptionally well all season. Up front we have Derren Williams who on his day will score goals out of nothing and frightens the life out of the opposition with his pace and power. He scored all three goals in our cup final win over Ixworth.

Alf Hicks reports on another 'team activity': the Annual Parish Meeting of the Parish Council, now in its centenary year.

Opportunity knocked for the 900 or so inhabitants of Wickhambrook one recent Thursday evening when the Annual Parish Meeting was held in the United Reformed Church School. A chance to come along and express their opinions. Did they come? No, only 25 of them. Either the village people are satisfied with their Parish Council or could it be that they could not care less!?

All seven Councillors were there.

(Three are local born and two have lived in Wickhambrook for over 30 years. With the other two having lived in the village twenty and twelve years respectively, this is seen by many as a good balance.)

Mr Peter Bayman was again elected Chairman and he nominated Mrs Brenda Fairhall as Vice-Chairman. This was carried. Other Councillors present were Mrs Thelma Farrow, Mr Colin Bird, Mr Jeff Claydon, Mr Robert Jones and Mr Steve Taylor.

... A report was given on the Charities Funds and Mr Colin Bird gave a very impressive statement on the hundreds of pounds that had been raised for the Surgery. It had helped in acquiring new items and had increased the facilities.

... In a comprehensive report on the work of the Parish Council, Mr Bayman said the aim of the Parish Council was to support and make things better for parishioners. It had to deal with planning matters and although it did not have the final word, the Parish Council played its part for the benefit of the village.

It was the custom of the Parish Council to make an award to

couples who attained their Golden or Diamond Weddings. The most recent beneficiaries had been Jim and Ivy Mayes who, with the help of their daughters Barbara and Linda, run the local combined post office, petrol station and shop.

November 1994

These extracts from the 'Wickhambrook Scene' have now covered the changes in the village over more than 25 years and, through its readers' reminiscences and historical researches, given us a glimpse of West Suffolk life over several centuries.

Let this chronicle approach its end with a nostalgic report on the return to the Normandy beaches from one who served both his country and then the village of his ancestors, which he came to almost by chance. And let it conclude with the poignant recollections of an elderly lady trying to come to terms with the changing face of Suffolk.

In March of this year I received, and gratefully accepted, an invitation from the Veterans of the 1st Battalion Suffolk Regiment to accompany them back to Normandy on June 6th, the 50th anniversary of the landings.

Leaving Bury St Edmunds early on 4th June the party travelled by coach to Portsmouth. We embarked on the cross channel luxury Brittany ferry 'Normandy'. Arriving at Ouistreham six hours later, we were met by coaches and then had to drive 50 miles to Flers, which is to the south west of Caen.

The following morning we attended Flers Memorial to the Dead, which was held in the town square, followed by a reception in the 'Mairie', a magnificent moated Chateau situated in the town centre. Here a further surprise awaited us veterans by being presented with an illuminated plaque commemorating the 1st Battalion's capture of Flers.

We then departed to go back to Colville Montgomery near the beach for another reception followed by a march to Hillman – a memorial to the Suffolk Regiment which was one of its first objectives, taking some 350 prisoners out from the underground bunkers. At this point we were presented with the French Normandy Medal and the Beauvielle Medal (Pegasus Bridge) and another illuminated certificate from the Province of Normandy.

On the 6th of June we again bussed to a national service at the cemeteries of Hermenville and Douvres-la-Deliverance at which the Princess Anne officiated. This was followed by the journey to Arromanches to take part, on the beach, in the veterans (8000) march past before Her Majesty the Queen. This proved to be a long and arduous wait of three hours whilst we were being regimented into columns of six for the march past. Getting off the beach was another three hours.

153

The following day, 7th June, our last engagement was the unveiling of the memorial to the men lost at the Chateau-de-la-Londes which was erected from subscriptions from the veterans and the site given by the present owner of the Chateau.

Being a gunner I was very honoured to have taken part in this trip. As an Air Observation Pilot Royal Artillery, we supported many units in those early days, including 51st Highland Division, 6th Airborne Division, and two Canadian Army Divisions with whom I was with until the cessation of hostilities near Emden in Germany.

I was asked how well the French had organised the whole anniversary. It was done absolutely marvellously considering they were celebrating liberation and we were commemorating our fallen heroes. They also suffered tremendous losses from our own air raids on both Caen and Flers.

It was all a long, long time ago but memories linger on and: 'We will not forget them'.

John Long, Ex Capt RA

CHANGING SCENES – *submitted by a lady who signed herself as 'D.H.' but whom we believe was Mrs Dorothy Hurrell.*

As I lay awake, having been disturbed by lorries thundering by in the stillness of the night, I drifted not into sleep again, but into the past.

I remembered when the main road outside with its heavy fast traffic, and now naked uninteresting verges, was a narrow country road. It was flanked with a row of beautiful poplar trees with fluffy seeds floating down like snow in spring. They straddled a deep ditch with its own beauty of wild flowers, frogs, newts, and butterflies, opening out to a small stream with a bridge over it to the fields and allotments. In my reverie it is now 6.50 a.m. I can hear the wind rustling in and out of the silvery poplar leaves and whistling through the telephone wires. The brook is gently rippling over the stones, the birds are singing, a cockerel crowing and a hen heralding the arrival of an egg.

Arthur Hurst is coming up the road coughing at each step. He is now as far as the 'stack yard' and 'Shacker' on his bicycle is the next sign of morning life. At 7.30 a.m. Brookes' men are on their way. 'Morning Bill', 'Morning Will', comes the reply as Dad goes out of the gate to begin his day.

Oh dear, I'm afraid I cannot see to write anymore. It must be because I am tired, or is it tears of nostalgia? The 'Thoughts of a Country Girl from Bury Road'?